The Best Intelligent Investor

Beginner's Guide for a Foundation in Personal Finance, Wealth Creation, Mutual Funds & Dividend growth investing. Trading Psychology, Cost Management, Tax Free Wealth

Bourke T. Johnsen

Table of Contents

Introduction

Congratulations on purchasing this book, and thank you for doing so. The world of finance is intimidating for most and may seem complicated or beyond our reach. Fear of the market, the risks involved, and not being properly informed about its functioning keeps most people away from the world of finance. These same people could have benefited from it and created their wealth. This book will help you understand the world of investing and the gifts it has in store for you.

One of the biggest impediments in investing that people face is the total absence of money to invest. Most people sincerely believe that they don't have the resources to make investments. They feel they are living day to day financially. They might be doing well for the expenses they have but have nothing to spare. Living paycheck to paycheck, they find themselves incapable of saving and investing. If you can relate to that situation, this book is just for you. It will help you develop a fresh perspective on investing and enable you to find the resources for investing that were always there.

This book is also a comprehensive guide for the more fortunate ones who have resources available for investing but are not able to pinpoint the correct place to invest. It will help you find the right investment vehicle that can take your investment places and grow your wealth.

When I say a comprehensive guide about investing, I also mean that this book will help you understand investing inside out. You will get to know the risk and rewards associated with investing. It is a great way to create wealth, but it may not be everyone's cup of tea. This book will help you understand whether you are cut out for investing or not. It will also give you direction to learn to invest if you haven't done that before.

It will serve as a primer for the new investors who have just begun their working life. For them, this book will open a door of opportunities and show a path to true wealth creation. If the direction shown in the book is followed, they will have a financially secure, stable, and comfortable retired life with all their financial goals in sight, regardless of the ups and downs of investing.

This book will give you a detailed insight into various investing instruments and the way they perform. It will also help you understand the science behind investing and the way it helps your money grow magnificently.

It will also explain and simplify the complicated concept of taxes and the way they can eat up your wealth. Not only that, but you'll have the information to help you survive taxes using your available resources.

From managing your cost of investments to remaining efficient, this book will prove to be a very helpful resource with every step of your investment planning.

Within the text, we'll try to debunk the myths most beginners have about stock market investing. We'll set a clear and defined path so that losses on investments can be avoided.

This book has been written in a very simple and easy to understand way so that everyone can take advantage of this information.

I hope that you will be able to take full advantage of this book.

There are plenty of books on this subject on the market. Thanks again for choosing this one! Every effort was made to ensure it is full of as much useful information as possible; please enjoy it!

Section – I
Are You Ready for Investing Money?

Chapter 1: Investment- Do You Understand the Term?

'Investing' is a word that can leave a sour taste in the mouth of many millennials. Most people living paycheck to paycheck may even scoff at its reference and ask about the availability of money for investing. Apathy is natural as a large number of people are not even able to get out of the vicious trap of payday loans. Their pockets dry out much before the next paycheck is expected. They borrow money on short-term loans at hefty interest rates and processing fees.

However, not everyone is living paycheck to paycheck. There are many people who are earning well above their needs. But, they have a completely different understanding of investment. Many such people do not see the clear difference between investing and trading. Most of them even think that putting money in their bank accounts is also a good financial decision.

Others want to enjoy it. They want to spend all they have enjoying life now and don't want to bother with plans for the future. For them, money is nothing more than just a way to get maximum pleasure out of life.

Then there are the prudent and financially responsible ones who want to save but hit a wall. They think that they don't earn or save enough to make a worthwhile investment.

The simple fact is, the world is made up of all kinds of people. Hence, there is no reason to judge anyone based on their financial preferences and understanding. However, one thing is clear. A large number of people do not have the required clarity and understanding of the important concept of 'Investing.'

A common reason many people are not very keen on investing is not their ability to invest, but their ignorance about the idea of investment in general and its advantages.

The objective of this chapter is to bring clarity to the concept of investing, what it means in real life, and why you need its benefits in your life.

The Idea of Investing

Let us consider the textbook definition of investing for the ease of understanding.

As per the Collins Dictionary, Investing is the simple act of putting money, effort, time, etc. into something to make a profit or get an advantage.

It means when you are investing your money, effort, and time in your education, you are investing for a better future as the knowledge earned in return would help you prosper. When you invest your time and effort into sports or any trade, you gain expertise. When you invest time in your relationship, you get love and affection in return.
Our parents invest their love and affection in kids so that the kids could grow to become capable members of society and make them proud. We invest in ourselves to

become better beings. We invest time and effort in our fields to get better yield and flowers.

The example above was just to explain that investing is nothing new to us. People become more aware when it's about money; otherwise, investing is part of everyday life.

If you are in any kind of job or get remuneration, then the money earned is disposable income. We call it disposable because it will get disposed of eventually.

Now, there are three main ways you can dispose of that income:

Spending: This is obvious. We all have some necessary expenses like rent, grocery, transportation, leisure, etc. Most of these expenses are unavoidable. There can be some expenses in these where there is no possibility of control or deduction while there are others where it is possible to make some adjustments. However, this is the bracket in which the money is purely meant to go out.

Saving: We all know about saving. It is the money or resources we put aside for the rainy days. Every individual can have a unique idea of saving. Kids like to put the petty change they get in their piggy banks. Some people like to keep small amounts of money in odd places like under the mattresses, in their cupboards, etc. Others like to keep the money in their banks. Irrespective of the location where you keep your money, it is supposed to be useful when you are in dire need. This money is your emergency fund that can be put to use the next hour, the next day, the next year, or may not even be needed for the next 30 years.

Saving is one of the biggest pieces of advice millennials may hear from their elders. The people who have been through the rainy days understand the meaning and significance of saving with greater clarity.

The concept of saving is very clear. Any money that you put aside anywhere for later use is your savings. It can be kept in your bank account, pocket, locker, or any other secret place.

Investing: Any money that is left after catering to your basic needs and saving for your immediate needs can be invested for the future. It is very important that you clearly understand the difference between saving and investment. While with both you are putting aside money for later use, you'll be able to use your savings as and when you need it. In contrast, the investment may not be available readily. Prematurely drawing out investments may even cause you a loss.

Investing means putting your money aside to buy or procure some assets with an expectation to get higher returns in the future. The view in investing is generally long-term, and that's why any attempt to withdraw money prematurely may not give you similar returns.

Key Differences Between Saving and Investing

Although saving and investing may look similar. There are five key differences between both.

Period

Saving is done with short-term financial objectives. Whereas, the financial goal in investing is generally long-term.

Your money can get locked in the investment for that period, and although you may own that asset, withdrawing money may not be possible before the term of maturity or premature withdrawal may even cause loss. If you are thinking of purchasing an asset in the future and you can't arrange for that money at once, saving is the way to go. You can put aside small chunks of money at regular intervals and then make the purchase when you have the full amount.

On the other hand, investing is done purely with a long-term perspective. The long-term for every asset may vary. There can be financial assets that may promise good returns in 3-5 years, while there can also be assets that may promise to multiply your investment several times over, but would need 20-30 years to bring results.

Therefore, the period of investment is an essential factor. If you think you'll be needing a certain amount of money shortly, you must not invest it somewhere. However, if you believe that there is a certain amount of money that you can spare and may be able to manage your expenses without, that money can be invested for higher returns.

Accessibility

Although we have covered this in the previous key difference, it is a significant difference between savings and investments. Your savings are like ready cash. For instance, if you have saved money in fixed deposits (FD) in any bank, it is as good as ready cash. If you need it urgently, you can break your FD and get the money. You may not get the full interest or any interest in the deposited amount due to premature withdrawal, but you'll certainly get your money. It isn't the case with investing. Many investments might have a lock-in period like government bonds, and that means that you can't get your money before the lock-in period. Other investments without a lock-in period may not be giving you good value at the time you need it. For instance, if you bought 1000 shares of ABC with a 20-year outlook, but need it after a year of investing, you may not even get the amount invested if the stock is trading at a lower price at that time.

Therefore, accessibility is another important difference.

Risk

Risk is the third most prominent difference between saving and investing. Saving is practically a safer option. When you save money in your bank account, it comes with the guarantee of the bank and the regulatory authorities that your money would be safe there.

The same is the case with the money kept in little stashes at home. It is guaranteed to be there unless someone steals it. There are no market risks involved with that money. Unless there is a burglary or a break-in, your money would be safe at that place for years.

It is not the case with investing. When you invest your money, you are putting your money to work. Every work has a percentage of risk. If the company, product, or service associated with the financial asset owned by you keeps performing well, the asset will keep increasing in value. But, if the asset is not performing well, the value of the financial instrument owned by you can even go down. Therefore, you must understand that investments are not without risk.

Let us understand it in simpler terms. Suppose you are studying for your graduation exam. You are investing your time, effort, and money in your education. You are even burning the midnight oil. But, unfortunately, you are not able to pass due to some reason. It can be due to poor preparation, more challenging questions than expected, falling ill on the day of the exam, or not having enough time to complete the exam. There can be several factors that may contribute to the failure, but the final result would mean a loss of time, effort, and money.

You invested your time, money, and effort in pursuit of passing the class. It would make your resume look better. It would make your chances of finding a better job easier. It is an investment and came with the risk of failing.

If you didn't invest, you could have saved on all that time, effort, and money. However, the saved time, money, and effort are also depreciative in value. There is a constant erosion in the value of your savings and that we'll discuss ahead in this chapter.

Returns

This is the star attraction of investing. The rate of return in investing is much higher than saving. There are several factors like the better performance of assets over a while, the compounding effect of interest, etc. However, you can be sure that although investing carries a certain risk, the returns are much higher than static savings.

Suppose your grandpa had put away a 1000 bucks around the great depression period in your basement. He would have made a great sacrifice. A $1000 at that time meant a fortune. But, if you find it today, would it mean the same to you? You can be certain that the only thing that grew on that money is mold. It is not going to increase in value.

Whereas, if a $1000 would have been invested and fetched even a 5% rate of interest, then in 91 years, it would value around $92,742.07, and that would certainly mean something even today.

Several investment instruments offer even greater returns. However, they also carry greater risk, and we'll cover it in detail ahead.

There are several long term investment vehicles like mutual funds and bonds that carry lower risk and excellent growth potential over the long-term.

The Objective

While deciding between saving and investing, the most significant factor should be your objective or the desired result. If you have short term goals and want greater liquidity, you should save that money. In that case, the money would remain readily available. However, you cannot expect the money to grow if you go that route.

In case you can manage to put aside that money for the long-term, you must invest it. The medium of investment can be chosen as per your risk appetite and reward expectation. If you want to keep the risk low, you can invest in government bonds and securities as they offer secured returns. If you have a higher risk appetite, you can invest in mutual funds, stocks, ETFs, and other such securities, and your returns can be much higher.

Let us simply consider the example of Gilead Sciences. The company has come in light recently due to the Covid19 Pandemic. There has been a surge in the prices of its shares due to the promise shown by the research of the company. However, it has been in the business for many years and has been making progress at a steady pace anyway. If you had invested $1000 in Gilead 20 years ago, the value of your assets would be around $76,000. This is at the current market price. The price was even much higher a few years back, but as an investor, you don't look for peaks or don't make an abrupt exit. Nevertheless, the increase in value is more than 75 times.

The simple fact is that if you invest and remain patient but watchful, your money would grow much faster than what you could have expected with saving it in a bank account. The latter will just increase marginally.

Why Is Investing Better Than Saving?

I'd like to begin by admitting that this question is flawed. Investing and saving are two different mediums to put money away for future use.

While saving is a safer medium with higher liquidity, the goal of saving is just to cater to the short-term goals. Saving helps you only in preserving the nominal value of money. This means that if you saved $100 today, it would still be $100 a year after, a decade after, or even after a century. However, the purchasing power of those $100 would keep going down with time.

If you consider the earlier Grandpa example, it's easier to understand that a fortune that Grandpa saved in those tough times wouldn't mean much today just because the nominal value of that money has come down.

Therefore, investing is a great option if you are looking for these two objectives:
1. Protecting the purchasing power of money
2. Growth in wealth

Protecting the Purchasing Power of Money

This is a factor that most people overlook. Just like we lose vigor, vitality, power, and strength with time, the same is also happening with money. If you have some money sitting idle, it may not remain that powerful after a decade.

Think of the things you could buy with $10 in your childhood and think of the prices of those things today. The price of most of the things would have increased, but the money saved by you is stagnant. Hence, it is losing value. This is called inflation.

When you invest, you are counterbalancing inflation. Your money also grows at a similar or faster pace than inflation, and hence your purchasing power remains intact.

Growth in Wealth

This is another essential thing that makes investing so important. We all know the limits of our working age. Some people will remain working for a bit longer while others may have to retire earlier. But, we all need to call it quits at some point. That would be the time when the money would stop pouring in. However, the expenses remain there and even increase due to the medical expenses of old age and other needs.

Therefore, at an age when you are not getting money, your need for money is expected to go even higher. You can't expect to get into a business or any other endeavor at that stage. You've worked all your life. Your retirement is for enjoying time in peace. But, for that, you'd need money. This is where investments can help.

Even small amounts that are appropriately invested can help in seeing big returns later on.

These are the two main reasons why investing is a great choice for all those beginning their careers or who are still at a young age. Such people can invest with great comfort and take more risks.

A person at a ripe age cannot afford to take more risks since the advantage of waiting for longer is not available. This is the reason that the manner of investing and the type of securities chosen vary a lot with the age of the investor, the risk appetite, the amount that can be invested, the financial goal, and the time at hand.

This book will help you understand all of these factors in detail and help you in becoming an investor who will be able to make informed and prudent decisions when choosing the best investing option.

Chapter 2: Identify Your Financial Temperament Before You Begin

As we all have a personality, we also have a financial temperament. Some people are spenders and don't mind trying to live well above their means. Then there are the cautious ones. Others understand the value of money and believe in conserving it to create wealth.

These can be divided into numerous categories based on their spending habits. However, three major classifications can help you in understanding your financial temperament, and you can begin improving from there.

The YOLOs: This is a common category. The young generation is a fan of this thinking. They grow up thinking that **Y**ou **O**nly **L**ive **O**nce, and hence saving and investing is a futile activity for them. On the contrary, they try to live well above their means. It is simply an attempt to taste the forbidden fruit.

These people are living on their credit cards. There is no liquidity. They don't have the cash. For anything they need, they are dependent on their credit cards. However, this is not a sustainable way to live. There are phases when job losses occur, there are extra financial burdens, and this causes payment failures as there is no saving to pay off the bills. Such people are in a constant pursuit to live a life they can't afford. They want to go to the best places. They want to have the best clothes. They want to throw the most happening parties to remain relevant in the circles they don't belong to. All this puts a very heavy burden on them, and they are the easiest to fall apart.

A very high number of youngsters try to follow this lifestyle, but thankfully most of them become a little more responsible in their middle ages. Unfortunately, by then, it becomes very difficult to be able to create wealth. They lose the prime of their life in which they had the opportunity to sow the seeds of wealth and see it flowering effortlessly.

The Balancers: These are the ones who are not getting enough to have everything they need, but they are managing to get what they need. The easy way out is to live on EMIs, loans, and mortgages. Although they are not trying to live above their means, they have high expectations and limited resources. If you look closely, a very large population falls in this bracket.

We want to have everything that is being advertised on the TV and the internet, but we don't have the resources. We find an easy way out. We start taking them on EMIs. We pay off the share every month, and hence we can have most of the things we need without having to wait for the complete amount of the resources.

These expenses are easy to justify as everything you buy has some utility. However, we all know that most of the things bought or replaced in this manner could have been avoided. We buy them because we can without having to fall into the debt trap. We can pay off the installments without feeling the pinch. This might sound like a sustainable model because it is aggressively advertised so by the banks and other lenders, but it isn't.

Most of the things we buy in this manner have no long-term value. We are just creating future garbage and not any value. Nothing of this sort could bring us money when we need it in the future. At least, it will not get you the money that was spent on it. Therefore, in your advancing age or in times of distress, when you need financial support, all these things would become a burden.

All your life passes in balancing the EMIs and your needs, but when you need money for big expenses like a college education for your kid, retirement, or medical emergencies in old age, there is no money to be used.

This is a less dangerous way to live life, but it is neither good nor very responsible. When we are earning, we not only need to think about our present but also about our future. There needs to be a consideration for the rainy days when we will not be in our prime to make the best of the moment.

The Makers: These are the people who live their lives responsibly. They understand the value of money and what even small contributions in the long-run can do. They start saving and investing early. They spend money cautiously on the things that are important and avoid the things they don't need.

You can call them minimalists, misers, pinchpenny, hoarder, saver, or uncle Scrooge. These are the people who understand the value of wealth creation and the way to do that.

They don't feel the need to show off their wealth for the world to recognize because they know that they have it. Most billionaires in the world fall into this category. They understand the true value of money.

These people make wealth from scratch. They save whatever they can on time and keep investing and reinvesting that amount into areas where they can get more profit.

Even simple conservation that is done with dedication can lead to the creation of wealth.

Now, you can be from any of these categories, and it is not very hard to figure out which category you belong to. However, the important part is to identify your long-term goals and bring changes to the way of your life. It doesn't matter if you are also a YOLO. You don't need to become an ascetic because that is not practical and possible for most people. However, what's possible is a course correction.

You can adopt some simple measures and bring a change in the way you spend money and conserve it. It doesn't matter whether you earn a lot or very little. You can still save some and start investing a little by adopting some financial discipline in your life.

Chapter 3: Things to Do Before You Get Your Feet Wet

Investing is a way of wealth creation. If you begin early and remain determined, just depositing $10 a week from the beginning of your working life until your retirement can help you gain more than a hundred thousand dollars. If you think that you must have saved that much by the deposits, you are wrong. Your total contribution would not even be a fifth of that. It is the compounding impact of interest that does this magic, and we'll discuss that in detail in the next chapter.

This chapter is about developing the mindset and discipline of investing. The fact is that there is a long way to go between thinking of investing and investing for real. It is one thing to get pumped up looking at the projected numbers after saving for a period of 20, 30, or 40 years and entirely another thing to do that consistently for that long.

Before you begin investing, you must learn to save money. You can't invest the money that you might need in a few days, weeks, or even months. Investing is a long-term affair, and numerous people fail to get that inside their heads. Some people remain confused between saving and investing, while others get confused between investing and trading. They hear about trading stories where traders make a fortune in a very short period, and they get pumped up to emulate the same.

You must understand it with clarity that success in trading is a rarity and not very common. Almost 70% of people who get into trading end up losing their capital within a year. Only less than 10% of people stay in trading even after five years of beginning. This should give you an idea about the way trading turns out for most people. The fortunate 10% of people that stay in trading don't just survive on luck. These are the people who devote their life to trading and understand analysis, charts, fundamentals, strategies, and have a lot of discipline. Yet, if you look at the average, the overall return in trading is less than 7-8%. When you compare that to investing, the average return over longer periods is generally above 10%, and that is visible with distinction if you look at the annual charts. To be precise, the annualized returns of the S&P Index from 1973 to 2016 were recorded to be 11.69%. This is far better than any trading returns over a long period.

Investing is a way of wealth creation. However, there are no shortcuts in investing. It would require you to keep investing and reinvesting with discipline. There would be times that you feel tempted to stop investing and indulge yourself in temporary pleasures. You'd also need to strike a balance between the expenses you need and the ones you can avoid.

To develop an investing mentality, you can begin by taking the following steps:

Learn to Get Over Paycheck to Paycheck Living

Most people would find the idea laughable as no one likes to live paycheck to paycheck by will. However, it is a misconception. We all have a choice. No matter what your salary package is, even the people earning in six or seven figures feel cash strapped. It is not the amount you earn that matters but the kind of expenses you have tied to yourself. The first step towards a responsible living is to manage your expenses.

Some expenses are unavoidable like rent, grocery, transportation, insurance premiums, etc. anything other than those can be managed as per your income. If you want to create wealth in the future, you must learn to live well within your means in the present.

Even the most well-off people in the world live frugally, and there is no shame in it. However, you may not want to live that way, and that's fine. But, you must ensure that your pockets don't dry up before your next paycheck is due. You must learn to manage your expenses in a way that

- First, you cater to your basic needs
- Second, you take money out for insurance premiums, savings, and whatever little amount you can for investing
- Third, you can spend the remaining amount on leisure

There may be times when you feel tempted not to take out money for the emergency fund or for investing, and this urge can only be controlled if you have your priorities right. That can't happen without learning to live responsibly.

Break the Burden of Paying High-Interest Debts

This is one of the biggest impediments people face in the way of saving anything. High dependency on credit cards, payday loans, and other easy credits also means that you'll have to pay a high rate of interest. Most people don't realize the simple fact that credit card companies and other lenders know very well. That fact is the inability of the borrower to pay off all that is due at once. This is the reason credit card companies offer interest-free money for a certain period and then charge hefty interests. Any person who is overusing credit will not be in a position to pay off the bills at the end of the month. Al least, not consistently, and credit card companies and other lenders benefit from this weakness. They charge exorbitant interest rates that will curtail your ability to save any money for investment or emergencies, and you'll keep sinking deeper into the debt trap.

Before you begin investing anything, you'll first need to get out of the high-interest trap and start taking out money for the emergency fund.

You must sit down to track the loans with the highest interest rates and then start paying it off first. Once you are done with that, focus on the other one. Getting free of high-interest rates should be your priority as they will keep sucking vital amounts of money out that you could invest for your future. It might take some time, and paying off high-interest debts is not as easy as it looks. You might have to sacrifice a lot of things, but it is essential to becoming financially responsible.

As you pay off a debt, you'll understand how light it feels and how easy it becomes to pay off others as the responsibility to pay interest would go down. You can only think of earning interest when you have paid off all the interest due.

You must understand simple math; usually, the highest rate of return you should expect from your investments would be in the ballpark range of 10%. Whereas the credit card issuers, payday lenders, etc. charge interest rates upwards of 18%. There is no way the math would work in your favor if you don't pay off your debts first.

Learn to Save for the Rainy Days

The third step towards becoming financially responsible is to learn to save for the rainy days. You must set up an emergency fund that should be used to cater to all the unforeseen expenses. These may include medical emergencies, unexpected costs that can't be avoided, and the expenses that you were expecting.

It is not the fund that can be used for investing. It is a fund that you must not touch except for the intended purposes. The purpose of this fund is to provide you cushion so that you don't feel tempted to look at your investments before maturity. The purpose of the invested money is to grow. It would mature in one instrument, and they may need to be reinvested until the final maturity time that you may have thought of. There should be no reason for you to touch the investments before the intended time. However, there can be times when you are in financial distress and may need money. The emergency funds cater to such specific needs.

You must make a habit to make separate contributions to the investment account and the emergency fund. These contributions don't need to be very big. Initially, you can also begin by just taking out a few bucks and putting them in the investment instrument of your choice.

It should be a part of regular practice every month. You must chalk out your expenses in a way that there is a section for the expenses, another for the emergency fund, and one for investments.

If you begin investing early, then you don't need to start with a lot. Even meager investments over a large period can lead to the creation of a good sum, and hence there is no reason for you to worry about that factor. Any fund that you set up at the beginning of your career will look hefty. However, this is just an early pain, and the things won't remain the same forever. Ten years down the line, your income would have increased, and the contributions will start looking small. At that stage, you can think of increasing your contribution and setting up other funds, like the contribution to your retirement funds, Roth IRA, etc.

Section - II
Investing- The Art and Science of Making Money Grow

Chapter 4: Carefully Understand the Magic of Compounding

The Miracle of Compounding Interest

As a kid, I always wondered why we could sow seeds in the ground and have fruit-bearing trees, but can't sow money and reap new bills every season—the money to buy as many toys and sweets as I wished. I was repeatedly told that it doesn't work that way. But today, as an adult, I know that it's possible to make money grow on its own. It won't grow on trees, but you can have your money planted in several other ways.

Investing is similar to gardening that can help you grow money from your money. You will need to save little chunks of money at regular intervals like you saved in your piggy bank in your childhood. You can have a whole lot more money at a fixed tenure which is also known as maturity.

Investing is an easy way to help your small contributions become huge.

For example:

If you begin investing only $10 a week at the age of 20 and get a fixed interest of 7%:

By the time you reach 30. You'd have invested $5200 in 10 years, the value of your investments would be $7448

If you look closely, $ 5200 in 10 years means $520 in a whole year. Around $40 a month. No matter how low your wages are, it is not a difficult target to achieve.

By the time you reach 40. You'd have invested $10,400 in 20 years, the value of your investments would be $22,079

By the time you reach 50. You'd have invested $15,600 in 30 years, the value of your investments would be $50,862

By the time you reach 60. You'd have invested $20,800 in 40 years, the value of your investments would be $107,482

As you can see, we have calculated marginal interest at 7%. Most investments would give you a higher rate of interest, and generally, it is calculated at 10%. I simply kept it 7% because I wanted it to sound as realistic as possible.

If you observe closely, this was the pocket change that you'd be contributing to, and it is easily possible to contribute much more than this. Even at that rate, the final amount at your retirement would be more than $100,000, while your contribution would be less than one-fifth of the total amount. Therefore, you can see the way your money has the power to earn you money simply by the magic of compounding interest.

Compounding interest has a magical effect on money. Your money grows at a slow rate in the beginning. You may feel in the first ten years that your money is just not growing at all. Then the next decade looks a bit promising, and after that, the addition is even more than the total money you have invested to date.

All this would happen without having to do anything extra. You don't have to walk an extra mile to take this money further. The magic of compounding is the main attraction that keeps all the millionaires and billionaires glued to the market.

All those people who think that all the rich people get rich by manipulating the market or making large trades overnight are reading too much fantasy stuff. Getting rich takes a lot of patience and perseverance.

People give examples of Warren Buffet and how he earned billions in the stock market. They fail to see that he started very early. He never invested money in buying physical objects which lose their worth over time. Whatever he saved and earned, he kept reinvesting it in the stock market, and yet it took him so long to get where he is today. People fail to realize that even Mr. Buffet took a very long time to reach where he is today.

Lionel Messi, the football sensation, was once called an overnight star. He replied that it took him 17 years and 114 days of tireless work where he started early and stayed late, day after day, year after year, to become an overnight star.

Success doesn't happen overnight. It is a result of hard work and perseverance. Through the stock market investment, you can reduce your work. You simply need to become perseverant as the money invested by you would undertake all the hard work, and you'll get the compounded interest.

Better Chances of Positive Growth

People remain skeptical of the market as they only see the regular ups and downs of the market. But, as I have already stated several times, if you look at the long-term stats from the standpoint of a steady investor, you'll see that the market has always shown a positive growth of around 10% every year.

In general, people new to the markets are curious, skeptical, and fearful. They hear stories about people losing all their worth in the market crash and become convinced that it is a black hole they must avoid at all costs.

There is always a struggle. Some people are always in favor of the market, while others are always critical.

There is nothing so black and white in this world. The world of finance is no exception. It has the potential of growth for your money if you follow correct investing principles and remain consistent with your investing habits.

At the same time, it is also a very dangerous place for highly risk-averse individuals with no financial understanding, backing, or experience and a desire to earn quick bucks.

If you have just begun earning and want to have stable earnings when you retire without having to do much about it, then you must begin investing little sums of money now. If you invest properly with a plan or diversified portfolio, you can remain confident that you'll have the money you are expecting when you'll need it.

Another big concern of new investors is whether they'll have positive returns from the market or not. You must understand that the market is always in a constant pursuit to go upwards. There are private and government entities that are working tirelessly to bring growth. This growth gets reflected in the market. If you look closely at the data of the past 8-9 decades, the market has shown steady growth. The average rate of growth has been around 11%. There have been decades when the market may have increased at a slower pace, but the market has always made up for the slow pace in good time.

Therefore, all you need to do is follow some basic and straightforward principles of investing explained in this book and watch your money grow with you.

Investing Is the Better Way to Beat Inflation

Trust is fragile. Most people find it hard to trust someone else with their money. It isn't very unnatural. If you put your money in someone else's pocket, you lose your freedom to use that money. An easier alternative to this problem devised by people is to keep that money safely hidden with themselves.

Now, I want you to imagine that one of your relatives lived a frugal life in the '60s and saved $5000. However, he had seen the Great Depression of 1929, and the banks closing up shop like nothing. For obvious reasons, he had no trust in the banking system, and hence he didn't deposit that money in the bank. He kept it safe in his home, hidden in closets so that the money didn't get stolen or lost. He died without an heir, and finally, his possession got transferred to you.

In the year 2020, you chance upon that stash of those $5000. You'd be elated to find some extra money. But would this be of the same worth it was for your grandfather?

You must understand that $4237 was the take-home of an average American family in those times. You could simply compare that money with the current take-home salary.

The cost of buying an average home then was $7,354. You could have bought a Volkswagen Beetle at $1280. Yet, your relative saved that money.

However, could you buy any of that money today? In comparison to the purchasing power of that money in the '60s, this money is worthless today. This is how inflation eats away value from money.

Now suppose that relative of yours had invested those $5000 in something that would have fetched him a steady return of around 8%.

He didn't need to do anything specific. Just put those $5000. In 2020, the total amount available to you would be $506,285.32. That is a figure that can make a lot of difference in your life.

Yet, the amount has been the same.

Inflation is the force that can erode the value from your money, and investing is an amazing way to save your money from its impact.

On average, the inflation rate stays steady at 3%. Some people may simply like to keep their money in their bank accounts as they don't want to deal with the so-called complexities of investing. They must understand that banks would give you a return of 3-4% while the inflation would be at 3%. Therefore, although the money would stay protected from the impact of inflation, it wouldn't see any significant growth.

Investing is a simple and effective way to make your money grow manifolds while you can enjoy your life without the trouble of managing it actively.

Chapter 5: You Don't Need to Be 'Wealthy' to Invest

Most people live with a misconception that they need to earn a lot to save for investing or that people with lower salaries can't invest. It is completely based on your perception. You could find numerous sports stars and Hollywood celebrities that had millions once but were forced to live in poverty or died without anything.

You don't need to be wealthy to create wealth. You simply need to be disciplined and committed to the creation of wealth. It is not your money or contribution that leads to the creation of wealth, but time. The longer you can leave the invested capital for compounding the interest, the greater would be the creation of wealth.

If you begin saving $100 a month at the age of 20 and keep doing it for 20 years, the wealth created would be more than double if you begin doing the same at the age of 40 but more than double your contribution.

Therefore, the most important thing in investing is not to invest a lot from the beginning but to begin early, remain consistent with your investing habit, and keep improving as and when you are capable.

You must make the fact clear in your mind that every individual begins modestly as an investor. The investors with grand portfolios didn't have that from the very beginning, but everything is just due to the magic of compounding.

When you keep your money in securities, it keeps increasing in value. The value of the stocks goes up. Some stocks split, and the number of shares held by you also increases. Several stocks give regular dividends, and if that value is also reinvested, your wealth keeps increasing.

Wealth creation is a magical and mesmerizing process that needs a push start in the beginning. However, once it starts rolling, it has its momentum to keep it going. If you thought that uncle Scrooge of the duck tales cartoon was mad about money without any cause, then you need to get there to feel it.

The feeling of money rolling in more money is just captivating, and once people have a feel of it, there is no reason for them to go back to their old ways.

Chapter 6: There are Easy and Simple Ways to Save Even on Meager Means

The saying is that where there is a will, there is a way, and that's completely true for investing. Given below are some of the ways you can find money to invest even when you have meager means.

Taking Out Money Isn't That Difficult

Investing is not about what you have but what you are ready to sacrifice. If you look closely, you would be able to find at least $10-$15 expenses in a day that you could cut down without any real effect on your life. It could be cutting down a drink in the bar, eating out, going for a movie on the weekends, or other such activities that could be supplemented in other ways and leave no impact on your life. However, the $10-15 saved every day would give you $300-$450 a month that could be invested. We have already discussed what a contribution of a paltry $300 a month for 15 years could mean in the long term.

Plan on a Fixed 10% Investment From Every Paycheck

The best way to make investing a reality is to treat it that way. Taking out money for investing shouldn't be an auxiliary activity but an ancillary one. No matter what you are earning, if you are not planning your expenses accordingly, then you are walking on the path of financial anarchy.

Whatever you are earning, you must cut down on some of the expenses and save at least 10% for investing. If possible, cut down more and invest more, but even if saving more is not possible, saving at least 10% is a good habit.

Do Not Fall for the 'I'll Do It Later' Trap

Most people think that they are young and they have their whole life ahead to save. They want to enjoy their youth completely, and the money they earn comes in handy for that. However, that's a misreading. The advantage of investing is in an early start because the time you have at hand is a more valuable asset than your money.

Let us get back to the earlier example.

You began investing $300. For 15 years, you invested that amount every month, and your total contribution was $54,000, and the total fund was $104,803 at the end of 15 years investing tenure. However, the real magic began after you stopped contributing to that fund. If you start investing at the age of 25, you could have stopped at 40. You'd still be in the prime of your working age, and hence there will be no need to use that fund, and it can be left for reinvesting or earning compounding interest, and within 30 years, it can grow to become a million.

But, if you began investing at 40, by the time you reach 55, your total fund would just be $104,803, and you won't have too much time left at hand to let it mature for the next 30 years. The magic of investing can be had by beginning early.

Keep Increasing Your Contributions

The standard amounts taken in the examples are just for reference. However, in practice, you must keep increasing your contributions as your earnings increase. You must understand that as your pay increases, inflation is also increasing at the same pace. While investing protects from inflation, if you don't increase your investment contribution as per your income, the outcome may not be as per your expectations. Matching your investment contribution to your pay increase is a habit that you must form at the early stages of your working life if you want to have a comfortable and early retirement.

If Possible, Go for Refurbished and Used Goods

If you're keen on investing and have a desire to save more and invest in your future, then you must go for refurbished and used goods as much as you can when possible. Most of these things are in great working condition and come at less than half the price of a new one.

This is a habit that can help you in finding ways to save while you try to meet all the immediate needs. This may not be possible all the time, but you will be able to save a lot of money if you give it a sincere try most of the time.

It is a fact that refurbished and used goods are also good for the money, and they can help you serve the purpose they were meant for.

Put an Effective Control on Overspending

This is the malice that plagues a large percentage of the population. Most people treat the limit on their credit cards as their own money. The fact is that you have to be careful even with the money that you have earned.

The more you spend, the more you owe, and not only that, but you feel motivated to spend even more. It becomes a habit.

You'd want to move on to a better car, better clothes, better places to dine in, better places to enjoy your vacations, etc. There is no limit on the better part. However, there is a limit to the money you can spend from your credit card, and then the cycle of high-interest rates would begin.

No matter how much money you earn, if there is a habit of overspending, you can drive yourself to poverty.

This is a habit that should be nipped in the bud. If there is a thing that doesn't count as essential, it is better to learn to avoid it. You must never forget that even Warren Buffet still drives a modest car regardless of his wealth and lives in the same home he bought in 1958.

Bring Down Your Cost of Living

It may not be possible all the time to bring down your cost of living since it can be impractical to move to the other part of the city just to cut down on rent. Especially since other costs would emerge like the transportation costs and the cost of lost time. However, there are several ways to bring down the cost of living, like choosing to bring down your eating expenses by cooking your food at home. It is a healthier and better option. You can learn meal prep, and that would even help you in saving cost and time both.

You can choose ways to bring down your travel costs and also the costs of leisure activities.

Find Ways for Creating Passive Income

This is a new world, and you need to evolve with this world to thrive constantly. The cost of living is increasing, and so are expenses. However, thankfully there are several ways you can have a little extra income without committing to those activities fully. It simply means that you can find ways to earn a passive income, and it can also help you in getting a steady income stream to invest for your future.

The objective of this chapter is to reiterate the simple fact that the only thing that can come between you and your financially secure future is your will to invest in a timely manner. The availability of funds is a secondary factor as we just saw that there are several ways that can help you in saving the little that you can invest in the time to get the funds you can be proud of in the future.

Section - III
Knowledge Is Power

Chapter 7: The Investment Options

There Are Plenty of Options

The general idea of investment for people is limited to stocks, bonds, and mutual funds. Although these three are wonderful products to invest in, they are not the only choices you have.

In the market, you also get other investment options like CDs, Index Funds, ETFs, IPOs, dividend stocks, fixed deposits, Roth IRAs, gold, real estate, etc.

There is no shortage of options that you have for investing, but there is enough lack of clarity and knowledge about these products. Most people still view investing as a complex function and try to stay away from it or prefer investing in mutual funds as they are actively managed by professionals.

There was a time when less than 2% of the US population took an active interest in the market and held any stake. However, that has changed drastically over the years because now more than half of US households have investments in the form of stocks, bonds, mutual funds, and other such products, and it is a welcome change.

You must understand that the world is running at a much faster pace. The potential of your expenses outgrowing your income is very high.

Even if that doesn't happen and you reach your retirement age without any problem, you'd face another hurdle of having higher expenses than income. It would be a time when you wouldn't be earning actively, but you may have expenses related to the college fee of your kids, loan repayments, and medical expenses of the advancing age. This is the age when your income should be higher than what you have been earning to date, but the opposite of that happens. This is where investing can help you.

You can invest in various investment options as per your risk tolerance and financial objectives by a predetermined time, and you can have an extra income that you may need at that age.

Choose Between Safety or Growth or Even Better, Find a Balance

Investing is a long-term commitment. It can't be indiscriminate. You don't invest just for the sake of it. It is a serious affair, and a deep thought must go in determining your objective of investment.

There are two main objectives:

1. Safety
2. Growth

Some people want safety from inflation and taxation, and that's why they begin investing. In contrast, others want rapid growth in their wealth. No matter what your financial objective is, as long as you have it in view, it is possible to plan and achieve it with investing.

Earlier, there were limitations in investing, and the options people had. The markets were very conservative, and the growth opportunities were limited. The availability of data was sparse, and people had limited resources to consolidate that data. This kept market information limited only to a few.

However, that's not the case today. Everyone has equal access to data, and research and statistics are also easily available. The markets have also come a long way, and a very high number of products are traded in the market that can give you great investment opportunities.

Earlier, you only had a choice between playing safe or going for growth. Now, even that has changed, and you can aspire for the best of both worlds by choosing to have a balanced portfolio.

This book would help you in understanding the importance of the proper division of assets and the way you can do that to get excellent returns.

Chapter 8: Understanding Stocks

Let us begin with the basics. Stocks are very simple. A stock is a share. When you buy the stock of any company, you buy a percentage share in the company's profit and loss.

The history of stocks goes back to 1602 when the Dutch East India Co. first issued its paper share to raise money for its overseas expeditions.

The Need for Issuing Stocks

When a company or entity needs money, it can raise money by issuing shares:

First, it can sell part-ownership of the company with others and raise money from it. In this method, whatever profit and loss it earns, it'll need to share that with the rest of the shareholders. Purchasing shares opens the door of having unlimited earning potential for the shareholders if the company makes a profit. However, it also exposes them to the risk of loss that the company might suffer while they still hold the share. This means that a shareholder is a party to the profit and loss of a company. However, the shareholders aren't liable to pay the debt of the company. Their liability is limited to the capital invested by them.

The ability of the stock to make the buyers a direct beneficiary of the profit of a company makes stocks so lucrative. However, one must not forget that the brunt of loss would also trickle down in equal measure to the shareholder.

Investing in stocks is an option since they can give you good returns even in short periods. However, retail investors must understand that they need to closely monitor the stocks as they can have rapid price movements.

Therefore, all types of stocks may not be suitable for investors.

Major Categories of Stocks

Large Cap (Big Cap): Companies with market capitalization higher than 10 billion are called the big cap or large-cap firms. 91% of the total US equity market comprises of such stocks. Most of the big US firms come under this category. Amazon, Apple, Microsoft, Alphabet Inc. all are large-cap firms.

This is considered to be a safer category for investors as these stocks are more stable and register slow but steady growth. However, an investor can never get complacent. The fall of a giant like Enron has taught that any company can fall, and it can be very complicated to predict the future of a company. Hence, even if you have invested in a large-cap stock, periodic monitoring of the stock will be a must.

Mid Cap: Companies with a market capitalization between $2-10 billion are considered to be mid-cap. These are the engines of the market. These companies have the growth potential and fire in their bellies. Stocks of these firms can give good returns if the company performs. However, the risk in these companies is also very high as they are in expansion mode, and companies usually crumble when they try to expand without a proper plan or backing. A high number of such firms end up accumulating excess debt and lower revenue that leads to their ruins.

Small-Cap: Companies with a market capitalization between $300 million and $2 billion are called small-cap firms. Like the mid-cap companies, they also have great growth potential, and they usually grow at a very fast pace. Small-caps stocks are especially liked by young investors as they can give great returns with a slightly higher risk factor. Institutional investors don't invest in these stocks due to market restrictions, and the stocks are played by individual investors. These stocks have the potential to outperform large-cap stocks in terms of returns. Opera Limited, Progress Software, PetIQ, and SailPoint Technologies are some of the leading small-cap stocks that have registered a good growth story.

Important Considerations for Investing in Stocks

These are the options that an investor has for investing in stocks. However, a very important point to remember is that retail investors must not rely too heavily on individual stocks as they will increase the risk in the portfolio too much.

When you buy the stock of an individual firm, your profit or loss will depend entirely on the performance of that company. Several things can cause a negative price movement in that stock, and your investment would have negative growth. The easy way out is to invest in the whole segment using ETFs or index funds and keep your holdings on individual stocks to a minimum.

If you feel that you aren't comfortable investing in index funds or ETFs, you can also invest in mutual funds that invest in stocks. They are also comparatively safer than individual stocks as they have a very diversified allocation of funds, and they can only invest in a certain class of stocks that are less risky.

Whatever way you choose for investing, you must not go the risky route. Having a diversified and balanced portfolio is a must for every investor, and we'll be discussing that in detail in the chapters ahead.

Chapter 9: Understanding Bonds

What Is a Bond?

A can directly borrow money by borrowing money on interest. For this, a company can issue bond certificates that would have a rate of interest and tenure predetermined. Irrespective of the profit or loss experienced by the firm, it would have to timely make the interest payments and return the principal amount at completion of the tenure. Bonds are free of the risk of profit or loss experienced by the firm. However, the rate of return for bonds is also limited to a great extent.

Characteristics of a Bond

A bond is simply a form of debt. The issuer raises money for a defined time frame and has to repay money to the lender at the defined date.

The fixed maturity date and a fixed rate of return are the defining characteristics of a bond, and that's what makes it so secure. A company issuing the bond will have to pay the principal amount after the maturity date has arrived. There are no exceptions to this.

The Main Categories of Bonds

Fixed-Rate Bonds: These are the steady bonds, and the rate of interest is fixed in these bonds. No matter what happens in the market, the lender would get the same rate of return.

Floating Rate Bonds: These bonds have a floating rate of return as per the prevailing market conditions. If the market is in an upswing, these types of bonds can bring more profit.

Inflation-Linked Bonds: These are inflation-linked government bonds that have a lower rate of interest than fixed-rate bonds, but in the long-term, these bonds can help the investor in remaining unaffected from the effect of inflation.

Perpetual Bonds: These are the bonds that do not have a maturity date. One advantage of investing in these bonds is that you can keep earning interest from these bonds for as long as you want. They do not come with a maturity date.

Portfolio Considerations Concerning Bonds

There is no doubt in the fact that bonds usually give a low rate of return in comparison to other financial products. But, they must be a steady feature of your portfolio because they give stability and security to your portfolio.

You can directly invest in your bonds, or you can also buy bond-based mutual funds. No matter how you want to approach this, having bonds is a must for a balanced portfolio.

You can devote some percentage to aggressive assets that can bring growth, but a big chunk of your investments must be directed towards security that promises steady returns over a long period so that you get the advantage of compounding interest.

Chapter 10: Understanding Mutual Funds

Mutual funds are among the most popular products in the investment category. Investors generally like mutual funds because they do not need to fret about the details as most of those are dealt with by the fund managers. They can just have their share and relax.

However, mutual funds are much deeper than that, and a poor understanding of the mutual funds can land you in deeper troubles. Most of the time, investors are made to pay more in terms of cost, fees, and charges just because they don't pay attention to the things mentioned in the prospectus.

Mutual funds may sound simple but are complex products. An investor must understand the exact securities held by the mutual fund and its type. The turnover rate and the costs of a mutual fund are also important factors as it is going to have a deep impact on your return.

Most financial advisors would approach you with their mutual fund products claiming that they have beaten all the records of the market, or they can help you get twice the returns you can get from the market otherwise. You need to be wary of such claims as most of the time, all that glitters is not gold.

What Are Mutual Funds?

A mutual fund is simply a company packaging various financial products as a whole and selling you a share in it. If you buy a mutual fund, you are buying a proportionate share of all the stocks, bonds, and short-term debts held by that firm.

The gist of mutual funds is in diversification.

Let us understand it in simple terms. Suppose you have $1000. You want to have a balanced portfolio. You want to include some large-cap stocks and bonds for safety and include several small-cap and mid-cap stocks for growth. Now, you can do that, and you'll need to spend a lot of time on that. You'll also need extensive knowledge of the products, and some products don't come cheap, and hence you may not even be able to buy that. This would leave your portfolio unsatisfactory and imbalanced.

A mutual fund is a simple solution to this problem. A mutual fund will have all these assets in a defined percentage, and you'll be able to buy a share of that as per your investment capability. Investing in mutual funds is as easy as that.

Buying mutual funds lowers your risk because you have a diversified investment, and they give a good rate of return.

Advantages of Buying Mutual Funds

Buying mutual funds has some of its unique advantages:

They're Professionally Managed Funds: Mutual fund companies take pride in the fact that their mutual funds are being managed by some of the brightest minds of the industry. The fund managers use all their knowledge and experience to manage the risk and growth ratio in the fund. They are continuously monitoring your fund, and whenever there is a considerable risk or an opportunity, the securities are switched.

They're Highly Diversified: One of the biggest advantages of buying mutual funds is that they are very diversified and hence carry comparatively lower risk. Even if one section of the mutual fund doesn't perform or has negative growth, other assets can balance that. The risk of the whole fund underperforming is very low.

They're Affordable: You can easily buy your share in a mutual fund and keep reinvesting as you like. They usually have a low dollar amount.

They Offer Greater Liquidity: Although there are limitations of time and certain restrictions on withdrawal too soon yet, almost all mutual funds offer the facility to redeem your share whenever you want against the net NAV. However, you'll certainly need to pay redemption fees.

Types of Mutual Funds

Money Market Funds: These mutual funds only invest in low-risk government securities. They are comparatively low-risk, but the rate of return of these funds is also proportionately low.

Stock Funds: As the name suggests, these mutual funds invest heavily in corporate stocks. The growth rate of these stocks can be high to medium, depending on the type of stocks selected. If the mutual fund is investing in growth stocks, then the dividend return may not be high, but the overall financial gain would certainly be high. If the mutual fund is investing in income, then it would invest heavily in the stocks that pay regular dividends. Some mutual funds invest in the index funds, and they mimic the performance of the index as a whole. Then there are sector-specific funds that specialize in a specific sector like the IT sector, automotive sector, or telecommunications.

Bond Funds: These funds invest primarily in bonds. The performance of various bonds then gets reflected in the performance of the fund.

Should You Invest in Mutual Funds?

This question can't have a straightforward yes or no. Mutual funds are good products, but they are not without cons. If you look at the performance of the mutual funds in the market, some have much poorer performances than various index funds and ETFs.

Another bone of contention is the fee and charges of mutual funds. You must understand the fact very clearly that mutual funds are expensive. There are a lot of costs that are levied on the shareholders. Hence the overall return promised to you at the time of investing in the mutual funds gets eaten up by these costs. We will discuss these mentioned hidden costs in detail in the chapters ahead.

Taxation can be another issue that may cause trouble if you are investing in some mutual funds that have a high turnover rate and unrealized capital gains. We will also discuss this part in detail in the future.

Therefore, when you are just starting investing, mutual funds can be a good choice, to begin with, as you can easily invest even with low capital and keep increasing your stake at a steady rate with reinvestments. However, once your portfolio becomes sizable, it could pay you more to invest in more cost-effective, simple, and better growth based products like index funds and ETFs.

Chapter 11: Understanding Index Funds

What Are Index Funds?

Index funds can be the most interesting addition to your portfolio. To keep it simple, even index funds are also a sort of mutual fund because they pool in money from investors to buy stocks that mimic the progress of the whole index.

In short, when you buy index funds, you are essentially purchasing a part of the whole market. This might sound counterintuitive because most funds are continuously trying to beat the market and over perform. However, there is enough data to suggest that over a long period, the indices always outperform various mutual funds. The best thing about index funds is that they have low management costs, and they are very simple to understand.

Things You Must Know About Index Funds

They Give You an Opportunity to Own the Whole Market: This is the best thing about the index funds. They buy stocks from all companies in that particular index. The purchase is made proportionately. However, this gives the retail investors the advantage that they get to buy the shares of even those companies that are very big and cost too much. The objective of the index funds is to mimic the performance of the whole index. Therefore, whenever the index gains, which it is bound to do at regular intervals, the investor gets a share of the gain.

There Is No Attempt to Beat the Market: Most mutual funds are continuously trying to beat the market in terms of growth. They get successful at times but also fail miserably many times. The result is directly reflected in the net worth of the investor. The index funds are not trying to beat the market. They simply follow the market in its footsteps and take advantage of its gains.

They're Getting Popular: The simplicity of design in the index funds is attracting investors in droves. They are getting increasingly popular because their cost is low, and the rate of return over time is good.

What Makes Index Funds So Effective?

No Sales Commission: Mutual funds come with a high front load fee that can be as high as 4-6%. You'll also be asked to pay a fee at the time of selling. Then several other charges eat your returns. Index funds A large part of your return that looks brilliant on paper is eaten by commissions and fees. You are only left with a minor profit, and then you have to pay taxes from your pocket, and that would be calculated on the total amount. Index funds are much better in this respect as there are no sales commissions.

Low Operating Expense: Most mutual funds charge high maintenance fees because they hire big fund managers. Their expenses are silently deducted from your overall balance. The expense ratio of mutual funds is much higher as they are also continuously trying to outwit the market, and hence frequent buying and selling of assets are required. This also increases the brokerages and commissions. Thus, the operating cost of mutual funds increases. This is not a problem faced by index funds as they simply need to mimic the indices. Hence their operating cost is low.

Tax Efficient: There is very little turnover in index funds because they are simply trying to follow the respective indices. In contrast, mutual funds are aggressively buying and selling assets to outperform the market. This can lead to a turnover of up to 200%. This will add up the taxes and brokerages. If the fund has unrealized capital gains, you could have another headache on your head. If you have kept highly active mutual funds in a taxable account, you could be in serious trouble.

More Diversification, Less Risk: The best thing about index funds is that they are as diversified as the whole index, and it can't get safer than that. Of course, there could be a time when the market is in a serious slump, but the market is bound to grow with time.

If you want to invest without worries and have an easy time, you can invest in index funds. These are highly diversified funds that work great with time.

When you go to buy index funds, it is very possible that you are offered index funds with front load charges and high maintenance costs. You must not buy such index funds. You must understand that there are people in the market with a simple objective of earning money from everything. However, there is no need to pay the high expense in index funds because there is a specific skill required in mimicking the market.

You must buy an index fund that does not have an annual expense ratio higher than 0.5%.

Chapter 12: Understanding ETFs

ETFs are also amazing if you want to invest in a whole segment without taking too serious of a risk. ETFs have stocks of the whole segment of the stock market packaged into one as a whole.

The best thing about ETFs is they offer the safety of mutual funds as they are highly diversified because they don't have just one or two company stocks but the whole segment. They also have good growth opportunities because the composition is only of stocks.

If you want to include stocks and feel highly optimistic about any specific segment in the market, you can go for ETFs.

The second best thing about ETFs is that they are not as expensive as mutual funds. The biggest problem with Mutual Funds is that their overall cost is higher as there are several fees involved in the form of the charges for the fund managers, consultancy firms, etc. For a small investor, this can pinch a lot as not a lot of money will go in stocks.

What Are ETFs?

Exchange-traded funds are open-ended securities. They comprise a basket of securities that can be from one specific industry or also from a range of industries. ETFs can also have other classes of assets like bonds and commodities too. These securities are used to assess the overall performance of an index, and you can trade them like stocks.

Let us assume that you are hopeful of the performance of the automobile industry in the near future. You expect it to go up rapidly. However, the major problem is that you are not sure about a specific company. Another problem is that you don't have that much to invest in the stocks of all the companies of that segment.

ETFs are a solution to this problem. They club industry-specific stocks together. So now you can buy ETFs that have invested in sports cars. There was a big range in which you choose not to invest as you weren't confident about them. You left out passenger cars, commercial vehicles, two-wheelers, budget segment, etc. Yet, you still picked up several stocks from an industry that might have required to shell out a lot of money.

The ETFs help you in this by clubbing various stocks together and giving the investors a chance to invest smaller amounts.

Advantages of Investing in ETFs

Diversification Lowers the Risk: Diversification is a word you'll hear in this book time and again. The reason is simple; only diversification is the guarantee of low risk. The more you feel inclined to keep all your eggs in the same basket, the closer you'll inch your portfolio towards risk. ETFs are a highly diversified product, even within the same sector stocks. Therefore, your risk is always limited. There can be times when a segment is under pressure, but the whole segment can't remain under pressure forever. Even if some companies perform, it'd be easier for you to save your investment, and if the sector as a whole performs well, your numbers can be great. The basic difference between Index funds and ETFs in this respect is of precision. The ETFs are even more precise because they are focused on specific sectors. Hence, the chances of growth are also higher.

The Cost is Low: Because the ETFs are also mimicking the whole segment, the cost of managing the ETFs is not very high. You can get them at a low-expense cost. Not only the management cost, but the purchasing cost of ETFs is also low as compared to the Index fund, where you may be required to buy bigger lots.

Easy to Trade: Another big advantage of having ETFs is that they can be traded just like stocks with the market hours. They have amazing liquidity, and hence you are always free to withdraw your money to invest in something else.

Tax-Efficient: The ETFs are also tax-efficient. The turnover of portfolio securities is low, and therefore you don't face high tax liabilities.

Types of ETFs

Stock ETFs
These types of ETFs track the performance of stocks in various segments. You can choose ETFs tracking large-cap, mid-cap, or specific industry or segment. ETFs can also be tracking segments globally. These ETFs give you the advantage of reaping the profit of specific segments in the stock market.

Index ETFs
This is the largest category of ETFs available. In this, the ETFs try to track the performance of the whole index. The index can be of any segment. For instance, you can have ETFs for indexes based on commodities and bonds.

Commodity ETFs
If you want to go long over the performance of various commodities, you can buy ETFs tracking the performance of various commodities. Previously, this was almost impossible for small investors as the commodities could only be purchased in big lots. However, you can now even buy Commodity ETFs for smaller denominations. Here, you will need to understand that the commodities market is highly speculative, and although your investment goes down, the risk in the market stays the same.

Bond ETFs
If you want to keep the risk of your investment low, you can start by ETFs that track bonds. In times of distress in the market, this can prove to be your best investment as the bonds rarely face market stress.

Forex ETFs
Some ETFs also invest in currencies, and if you want to speculate in that area, these will give you a chance to do so.

The risk to reward ratio in the ETFs is high, and they also give a small investor to test the large segments which were unapproachable with lower investments. ETFs open a level playing field for you, and if you want to take a risk, you can do so. However, they also give you the option to play safe and invest your money in a diversified fashion.

As a beginner, you can give ETFs a chance as they present reasonable wealth creation opportunities and also help you in saving tax.

Chapter 13: Understanding Dividend Stocks

Passive income is a tempting term. Most people are stuck with their fixed-income jobs but desire an additional source of income. This is a want that has been in the heart of people forever, and it is a reason fake pyramid schemes and multi-level marketing scams work all the time despite regulatory warnings.

However, dividend stocks can give you a genuine way to earn passive income. An income that will be truly earned, and no one would be doing a favor giving that to you.

The dividend is a kind of reward several companies give to their investors for investing in them. It is a form of cash reward given to the shareholders periodically.

Here, some things should be understood clearly at the very beginning so that there is no ambiguity.

- There are several companies with a sound track-record of paying dividends
- Even those companies are not bound to pay dividends
- There is no rule stating a company will have to pay a dividend
- It is a way devised by the companies to reward their shareholders for their loyalty and investment
- Companies can pay dividends monthly, quarterly, semi-annually, or annually
- A portion of the company's profit is given as dividend
- It can be given in the form of cash
- Additional shares of the company can also be given to shareholders as a share dividend
- Sometimes, companies also give special one-time dividends to reward the shareholders on major occasions

Advantage of Buying Dividend Stocks

The biggest advantage of buying dividend stocks is that you keep getting some return on your investment without taking out that investment. This amount can be reinvested into that stock, and your investments would keep increasing.

The share dividend isn't a very big amount if seen in value for each stock. But, when you build a big portfolio over a while and have a good volume of stocks, this dividend amount multiplies and becomes handsome.

It is simply rewarding to see your money coming back as profit and getting a chance to reinvest it.

Do All Companies Pay Dividend?

No, not all companies pay a dividend. A dividend-paying company should not be your standard for choosing the right stock. Alphabet, the parent company of Google, doesn't pay a dividend to its shareholders. However, it is clear about its reasons for not doing so. It states that it can reinvest the money better and add value to the company and stock prices much better than tohe stockholders could do with the dividend paid out at regular intervals. Several other high-profile companies also work on that same belief.

Should You Choose Companies That Pay Regular Dividends?

This is a question that you must be asking yourself. If you are the kind of person who likes to see his/her investments grow, you'll like the dividend stocks. If you have developed a taste for compounding interest and know the magic, it can work upon the overall investment, and then also dividend stocks can be a lucrative option for you.

However, if you may not feel inclined to put the dividend payouts back to the investment to grow further, then these stocks may not hold much value for you. In that case, you should look towards investing in stocks that are doing value addition to the stock on their own.

If the idea of compounding the interest ignites a fire in your belly, then dividend stocks can be a good option for you.

Here, you should also understand that shareholders can also reinvest their share dividends directly into the stocks of that company without having to buy shares through the regular channels. This can be done through the Dividend Reinvestment Plan (DRIP) run by that firm.

Chapter 14: Understanding IPOs

Initial Public Offering (IPO) is the process through which a company issues its new shares to the public for the first time. IPOs give public investors a chance to invest in new businesses.

Why Do Companies Issue IPOs?

Initially, companies establish themselves on their own. They build a structure and business model. It can be a family-owned business or a business started by a few individuals. However, every business needs money for expansion. This money can be raised through loans and investments. Businesses can take loans from banks and other lenders. Angel investors and venture capitalists can also fund profitable businesses for a percentage stake in the company.

When the company wants to expand further, it would need more money. The angel investors and venture capitalists may also like to realize their profits by selling a percentage of the shares owned by them. For this, the company may choose to launch its IPO and sell a percentage of their shares to the public and raise money.

It is a way for the company to raise money. This money can be used for paying off previous debts, future business expansions, and even raising money for the promoters.

The way this money is to be realized has to be mentioned in the prospectus issued by the company for the investors.

Bringing an IPO means that the promoters would give off a percentage of their stake in the company. IPOs can be a good opportunity for small investors to gain stakes in a company at the same price as institutional investors and high net-worth individuals. Everyone gets the shares at the same price in an IPO.

Can IPOs Give Small Investors a Chance to Earn Money?

The short answer is that through IPOs, companies offer their shares to the public, and hence they can be used as an investment tool. Therefore, you can earn money through IPOs.

However, there are several misconceptions that the general public has regarding IPOs that need to be cleared.

It has been seen that many IPOs climb rapidly at the time of listing. Therefore all the individual subscribers who had applied for the shares get a chance to earn good profits from the sale of those shares. This is a reason many people believe that IPOs can prove to be a sure-shot way to get rich fast.

As I mentioned earlier, this is a misconception. All IPOs don't climb at the time of their listing, and some IPOs may even perform poorly, and your money can get locked in them.

You cannot buy as many shares as you want through an IPO. In case the IPO is oversubscribed or overbooked, you will only get the shares proportionally. If the craze for the share is very high, then it might be given through a draw of lots to the applicants, and there is no guarantee that you'll get the shares in the IPO. Even in case you have been lucky to get a few lots of shares, and the share also performs exceptionally well at the time of listing, you will have profit, but that wouldn't be making monumental profits at the number of allotted shares wouldn't be much.

You must understand that good IPOs give you a chance to enter into a good company at reasonable prices. However, they must not be treated as an opportunity to make a quick buck if you want to think from the perspective of a long-term investor.

All IPOs don't perform well. IPOs hold a great risk for the investor as there is little knowledge about the company, and there is very little information publicly available. Once the company gets public, it will have to put its records on the table, and there would be greater transparency, but at the IPO stage, most of the things that you know are the things mentioned in the prospectus issued by the company.

There are times when investment banks and brokers create unreasonable hype about an IPO. This leads to overbooking of the IPO. However, this craze is generally short lived, and the prices come to their real value in a short amount of time.

Making money through IPOs is very much possible. But, you'll have to remain sensible and reasonable.

Some of the things that can help you in remaining profitable by investing in IPOs for the long-term:

Is the IPO Overpriced: If the IPO is overpriced, that would mean that the promoters are greedy, and they are trying to milk the investor. The prices of the stock can go down in the future as a form of correction, and hence investment in such IPOs is not good. Invest in IPOs that look undervalued.

The Purpose of the IPO: This is again a very important thing to look for by the investor. The company has to mention how the money raised through this IPO would be used. If the promoters plan to put this money in expansion, debt reduction, and other constructive purposes, then it would mean that there will be a value-addition to the company, and chances of success would increase. In case the promoters simply want to pay off the existing debts through this loan, then the IPO may not be very lucrative.

Fundamentals of the Company: This is the basic metric that you look for while selecting shares, and the same principle should apply to the IPOs too. The company would present its financials in the prospectus, and that can help you in judging things like debt to equity ratio, promoter holdings, cash flow, profit margins, etc. These things can help you in understanding the profitability of the investment.

Future in the Segment: This is another parameter that you must keep in mind. You must ask yourself whether you see a good future for that segment as you are going to invest in that company for the long-term. If you think that the sector would keep growing at a steady pace for the next few years, then only invest in it.

Remember, there are no lone-wolfs in the financial world. If that segment doesn't have prospects, leave it aside.

Don't Fall for the IPO pop: Many people invest in IPOs only because that IPO is garnering great attention, and hence the chances of the IPO gaining a great listing increase. This means that the investors can get a better price at the time of listing, and they can book their profits immediately. We have discussed it above. If the IPO is getting oversubscribed, then the chances of your getting a lot many shares are very slim. There is no way you can get rich through the margin you get from the sale of a limited number of shares. The more important thing is that this is a highly speculative game. This might be a lucrative thing for a trader, but for an investor, it wouldn't do any good at all.

Therefore, IPOs are a good way to take a position in good companies.
You get a chance to buy shares at a reasonable price. The chances of the price of the stock going up from there are very high.

Going long on financially and technically sound companies is a good investment decision.

However, IPOs have their inherent risks as most of the inside information about the company is still not in the public domain or under rigorous scrutiny. This does put your money at some risk.

You must weigh the risk properly before making an investment decision.

Section - IV
Getting the 'What If' Out of the Way

Chapter 15: Dealing With Information Overload

One of the biggest problems in this world is the problem of choice. Just knowing is not sufficient. Sometimes when you know a lot, and most choices look like good choices, making the right decision can become very tough.

This might not look like a very tough decision for you at the moment, but when you are about to make the decision:

- You will be surrounded by self-doubt
- You will have second thoughts about the better opportunities available
- You would feel inclined to invest in more tempting assets that can bring better returns
- You will feel fidgety

These are natural reactions, and you'll not be the first to have these thoughts. Most investors feel this chill, and it is natural.

However, the problem is that the anxieties you get can make you weak in your decision making, and you may not be able to form the right investment strategy.

Knowledge about the investment tools is one thing, and determining the right assets to put your money for objective growth is entirely something else.

You may find an investment opportunity to be the best, but:

- Can you be sure that it wouldn't fail you?
- Are you sure that these tools can help you build the type of retirement fund within the time frame you are expecting?
- Have you carefully examined the risk and covered it?
- Can you be confident that it would give you the expected results?
- Can you be sure that the options you are leaving out won't perform better?
- Will you be able to sleep at night with peace of mind for the whole time you keep your money invested in these securities?

You may think that most of the questions will take us towards speculation. However, when you are investing in a better future, these questions will have to be addressed. You can't put your life's savings into something that may turn out to be a dud in the end when you'd need it the most.

The best answer to all these questions is the selection of an efficient asset portfolio that has the right balance of safety and growth.

Every individual can have a specific idea about the right asset portfolio, and as you begin looking for investment opportunities, you'll encounter scores of people who'll present themselves as financial wizards. They'll show you investment portfolios catering to your specific investment needs while you are still in doubt about your needs.

This is a very common issue encountered by people, and they are made to think the thoughts the investment advisors have in mind. This is not the road you'd want to take.

Investing must be your informed decision because you'll be putting your life's savings on the line. No one will have a better view of your requirements and future visions. The objective of this chapter is to help you understand the basic parameters that should form the basis of your asset portfolio selection.

There are always some basic questions, and the answer to those questions may vary for every individual, however, knowing the answer to these questions will help you in determining the future strategy.

The purpose of this chapter is not to direct you towards a specific investment tool but to help you understand your long-term financial needs and the tools that can help you in addressing them.

Chapter 16: The Cornerstones of an Efficient and Targeted/Objective Portfolio

The heading of this chapter needed to be abundantly clear, and there is a great chance of misreading. This chapter is specifically about the principles for building a portfolio that would be able to cater to your objectives.

The main objective of any portfolio is to get higher returns with low risk. No one wants to take a higher risk for low returns. Hence, there is no question debating the need for higher returns. The question that we need to ask is whether you are ready to take the risk required to the returns you need and are you prepared for it?

The reason I made that statement is pretty simple. Most of us want to have high returns, but we all know that for high returns, you will need to take high risks. In the beginning, when you haven't invested anything, it seems pretty easy. However, once you have invested a substantial part of your savings and committed yourself for more, you begin to feel cornered, trapped, anxious, fearful, and hopeless.

The thought that you might lose money and the actual risk of losing money has completely different sensations. You may not be prepared for both at the same time.

When we begin chalking out an asset allocation plan, four very important questions must be answered with complete honesty. You must look for the answers objectively if you want to spend the rest of the time with complete peace of mind and surety in the heart.

1. What is Your Financial Objective?
2. What is the Amount of Time You are Ready to Stay Invested?
3. What is Your Risk Appetite?
4. What is Your Current Financial Standing?

If you answer these four questions with sincerity, you'll be able to allocate assets with greater clarity of mind and do complete justice with your financial objectives.

The world of finance has its uncertainties. Bad times can come calling without warning. However, if you have invested as per your financial goals and not taken unnecessary risks influenced by fear and greed, you can be sure that your investments will remain relatively safer.

Let us now understand these four questions and the impact they have on your asset allocation decisions.

What Is Your Financial Objective?

A clear understanding of the financial objective is very important. We have covered this topic even earlier in the book, and it will again spring back several times because this question is crucial to your whole investment planning.

If you need to save money within a few months or a couple of years, investing may not be a very prudent idea for you. For meet your immediate expenses, you must save money. Buying a car or saving money for your marriage are near-future goals and wouldn't allow you the amount of time needed for investments to grow to their full potential.

Most people get blinded by the projections of the financial world in the movies and begin thinking that if they can invest the money spare with them, they'll be able to make more from it. The general idea is correct, but the time frame is unclear.

You will have a chance to make a lot of money from your investments, but that money can get locked for a very long time, and you may not be at liberty to get it out as and when you want without having to face substantial losses.

Every investor must have a clear goal and a time frame for achieving that goal. If it allows substantial time to keep the money invested, then only you have the right opportunity to invest, or else you can start feeling trapped.

Another thing is a clear idea of the kind of money you are thinking of having in the end.

Although the rates at which you calculate your returns are tentative, they give you an idea about the kind of returns you can expect. You'd also get to know the amount of money you'll need to invest and the frequency of your investments.

You could be planning for your kid's college education, a world tour with your spouse, or a comfortable retirement with a hefty bank balance. Whatever you are dreaming of, you must have a clear objective in mind so that you can begin planning accordingly.
When you calculate your financial objectives, you'll also need to take into account inflation. The purchasing of $100 is not the same as it was 30 years ago. You shouldn't have any reason to believe that it'd be stagnant after 30 years either, and that should also be taken into account.

What Is the Amount of Time You Are Ready to Stay Invested?

Investing is done with long-term planning. However, the definition of the long-term may vary from person to person. For a day trader, waiting for a week with the securities in your book can mean a lifetime. This is because the day traders have very thin trading margins. Keeping securities overnight can mean the change in price can be huge when the market opens the next day, and the trader may lose a fortune.

To wait even for a few minutes while trading can mean a lot for the people who do scalping. They have the thinnest margins for trading, and their whole trading game relies on making a high number of trades at lightning speeds with ultra-thin margins. They rely on the volume of trading and not on the margin of trading.

However, an investor might stay invested in a specific asset for years or even decades without moving a muscle.

The difference in trading style comes from the trading objectives. The day traders and scalpers trade for their daily bread and butter while an investor buys assets with a future objective in mind.

Irrespective of the type of asset class you choose, investing will mean staying put in security for a certain period. Investing is not a way to get quick results. The main force behind investing is the effect of compounding interest. When you stay invested, you earn interest even on the interest you have earned, and that makes your gains even bigger.

Investing for shorter periods is a strategy that can easily backfire. When you invest, you have to overlook the usual market fluctuations. The assets may go up or down in valuation in the shorter range. However, that doesn't affect an investor because the assets are acquired with a long-term view. If you have a short-term view or objectives, your investing strategies would need to be completely different.

Let us suppose you have invested your money, and you are expecting an 8% return every year.

Now, suppose you invest $300 every month and get an 8% return.

If you invest for ten years, your contribution would be $36,000, and the interest would be $18,385.

If you invest for 20 years, your contribution would be $72,000, and the interest would be $99,798.

If you invest for 30 years, your contribution would be $108,000, and the interest would be $317,284.

If you invest for 40 years, your contribution would be $144,000, and the interest would be $828,541.

As you can see, investing projections are usually based on steady returns over a period, and they begin to peak as you give them time. If your view is short-term, investing in certain assets may not work for you. Your money would grow at such a slow pace, initially that you begin feeling frustrated.

If you look at the annualized returns of various assets, you'll find that long-term investments will give you a better opportunity to keep your money safe. You may get huge returns on some assets the very next year and may not get that chance for years. It heavily depends on market conditions. If you have time on your hands, you will be in a position to choose the time to take an exit with maximum gains at hand.

In the short-term, the fund may not be in its prime to give you any kind of return. It is also possible that the growth is negative. The money can remain locked for longer than you intend. Then there are issues like taxes and costs.

Several securities are good for specific time frames. If you have a specific duration in mind and do not mind settling for a lower rate of return, investing in bonds is a much better option. It is a safe and reliable option that comes with a maturity date.

If you'd like to get greater returns, you can invest in mutual funds. They'll give you an option to make an easy exit when you want, but you may not get the profit you are looking for at that time in case of a premature exit.

Investing in index funds and ETFs is also an option with you as they give steady returns over a while and are easier to manage.

All assets will give you a different rate of return as per the time you have at hand to stay invested. You must make a decision based on your ability to stay invested for that period.

What Is Your Risk Appetite?

We all want to make more profit and face no loss. However, this isn't how the money market works. A person's gain is another one's loss. There is no way to find a way that guarantees 100% success, or even close.

The world of finance is clear; the people who are ready to take more risks will have the advantage of earning more profit. If you are investing in a company as a shareholder, you have earned a right to share the success of that company. However, you are also at the risk of losing all your investment if the company fails.

In case you are simply lending to a company, you will have the right to ask for interest no matter if the company is making a profit or loss. However, this also means that even if that company strikes gold from the money you gave, you'll have no right to ask for a single penny more.

When you lent the money, your risk was low, but even your reward was limited. When you invest the money in the profit or loss of the company, you get to share the spoils of success and also the ruins of failure.

Although it may look easy, the decision is not simple. There is no reason for you to believe that the market will not behave unpredictably in the future. You can never be too sure about the performance of any company or asset.

If uncertainty makes you feel jittery, then you must only invest in low-risk assets. If you are young, you have time on your hands, and you are not afraid to take risks, you can invest a portion of your investments into high-risk assets that can fetch better returns.

The percentage of money that can be invested in high-risk assets and the percentage that should be put in low-risk assets would depend on the kind of money you can afford to lose without losing sleep.

Although you will have complete command over this money and you will maintain a watch over this money, it should be the money that you are completely comfortable losing. Losing money is never a comfortable idea, yet only that money should be invested in high-risk assets over which you don't lose your sleep.

You must sit down to determine the percentage of money from your monthly or annual contribution that you are comfortable putting into risky assets.

The risk is not without a cause. Given below is a table demonstrating the average return of various portfolio combinations and the worst annual loss registered by those combinations to give you a better understanding of the risk-reward ratio.

Fund Allocation	Average Return	Worst Loss in a Year
100% Bonds	5.5%	-8.1%
80% Bonds & 20% Stocks	6.7%	-10.1%
60% Bonds & 40% Stocks	7.8%	-18.4%
60% Stocks & 40% Bonds	8.7%	-26.6%
80% Stocks & 20% Bonds	9.4%	34.9%
100% Stocks	10%	43.1%

As you know, stocks are riskier than bonds. As the percentage of stocks in the portfolio increased, the average return also went up. However, the risk of loss would also go up accordingly. As your portfolio becomes more reliant on bonds, the rate of return comes down, but even the risk of loss also comes down.

This is a very simplistic representation, as these are only the basic assets that you can have. You have a combination of assets that provide you a better cushion against risk and also higher returns. However, the idea of risk must always be clear in your mind so that you don't feel restless once you have invested your money in an asset.

This is also very important because once you have invested your money, a premature exit can lead to a loss. But, if you remain invested, you might keep feeling anxious, distracted, and restless.

Therefore, a correct determination of your risk-appetite is very important. This anxiety gets even more pronounced when the markets are on a bear run, and your funds begin to shrink. It takes time and experience to develop an understanding that such phases keep coming and going. However, many people panic and start selling their assets, which can lead to substantial losses. This is the reason it is always advised that an investor must only invest in high-risk securities as per one's risk tolerance.

What Is Your Current Financial Standing?

The final part of your portfolio decision is to assess your current financial standing. Every investor will have specific investment needs and requirements. A person at the beginning of the career has a lot of time at hand and high risk-taking abilities.

Such a person can easily adopt a more aggressive investing approach and try to build a bigger investment portfolio. A person in the late 50s or nearing retirement would have most of the things needed and shouldn't invest in high-risk assets. Even if that person remains invested in assets that protect against inflation and some returns, that should be good enough. If someone already has a hefty portfolio, there would be little need to take unnecessary risks. At the same time, youngsters with no portfolio can take the risk to build a portfolio that can give them a good head start. They can also divide their investment in a way that a part goes towards safer investments, and another goes towards high-growth assets.

If you answer these four questions clearly, you'll be able to design an asset allocation plan that gives you the correct growth potential.

There are two main parts of an asset allocation plan:
1. Choosing Correct Investments Vehicles
2. Subdivision of the Allocated Assets

Importance of Choosing Correct Investment Vehicles

The world of finance can start sounding intimidating when you start listening to terms you have very little knowledge about, and believe me, there would come a time when you'll hear them most often. A high probability of that happening would be from the mouth of investment advisors who will be hellbent on selling the product they think has the highest potential.

In the beginning, the picture presented is always rosy, and you would be shown an image of comfort, luxury, and financial freedom, but that's a trap you'll have to learn to dodge.

Make it a rule to never invest in complex investment options no matter how well they are presented to you.

Hedge funds, gold bullion, unit trust, penny stocks, commodity futures, options, and several other such products are wonderful in their own right. They do have the potential for seasoned traders and investors. But, for an investor who doesn't maintain a hawk-eye on the market and has a deep understanding of the financial world, these products can become a financial graveyard.

Stocks and Bonds are two simple products that are easy to understand and maintain. You can get their numbers on your smartphone and read them in the newspaper. These are the instruments you must rely on.

Stocks: They are directly linked to the financial performance of a company, and hence they have high potential but also a higher risk percentage. This is a reason general investors must not rely heavily on any specific company for their investments. No matter how much you trust a company, never invest all your money in it. The better way to deal with stocks is to have a diversified stock portfolio. You can invest in several large-cap, mid-cap, and small-cap stocks. This will provide you a cushion against any specific problem in any one segment.

You can also invest in Stock Mutual Funds. They are managed by professionals and have a very diverse portfolio. This will also save a lot of headache on your part.

ETFs: If you have a particular liking of any particular segment like banks, automotive, IT sector, etc. you can also invest in ETFs as they help you in buying the segment as a whole and hence the impact of any particular company failing in that company will not have a deep impact on your portfolio. ETFs provide a great investment opportunity for investors who want to invest and forget about the regular ups and downs of the market. They are comparatively safer, and their overall cost is also low.

Index Funds: If you look at the data of the stock market, you'll notice a significant thing that the market has been rising on a steady basis. There have been times when the growth looked stunted, and some industries were under pressure, but the market as a whole has always outperformed all the other segments. Index funds give you a chance to invest on a broader spectrum and remain worry-free about the daily ups and downs of the market.

These are the investment vehicles if you want to build a stronger portfolio faster. Stocks have a higher risk and also a higher percentage of the reward. If you are young and have a long road ahead of you until retirement, you can have an aggressive portfolio with a greater weightage to stock products. Individual stocks are riskier, but when you invest in diversified products like mutual funds, ETFs, and index funds, you are not investing in a specific company but on a whole segment and hence the protection is better on a long-term basis. Data shows that segments as a whole generally outperform a specific stock in particular on a long-term basis.

Bonds: Through bonds, entities like government departments or companies try to raise credit for their functioning. Bonds are safer securities because they promise to pay interest on the invested amount and bear no risk of the performance of the entity in the future. However, that also limits the overall return or reward potential. But, as an investor, you must never discount the importance of bonds in your portfolio.

Bonds are securities that help in balancing your portfolio. They give it security and stability. The returns in bonds are slow, but they are safe returns.

If you are a young investor, your portfolio must be a little biased towards stocks but also must invest in bonds. If you are an investor with a good portfolio and have little time on your hands, you must not take the risk of relying heavily on the stocks, and your portfolio must be biased towards bonds and only have a smaller percentage of stake in stocks.

Subdivision of the Allocated Assets

When it comes to the subdivision of the assets, diversification is the key. Keeping all eggs in the same basket is not a prudent strategy, and we all have been taught this simple yet important lesson from a very young age.

Investments are exactly like eggs. The future is trapped inside the shell. All the eggs may look the same from outside, as they all have a hard shell. However, from the inside, an egg can be rotten, healthy, or may even have a chicken. There is no way to know that with complete surety. A severe jerk of the basket can crush the eggs, and if all the eggs are in the same basket, you'll have a great mess and a lot of regret on your hands.

Therefore, diversification provides you protection against such eventualities.

Within every class of assets, there would be certain products that behave differently. Not all bonds are equally slow, and not all stocks have the same degree of risk. Even in stocks, some stocks have a better potential of growth, while others may keep lying low for years at a stretch.

You must think that knowing which products would work would hold the key to magic, but that's far from being true. Not even the financial wizards can make an exact prediction about every investment they make. If you think that Warren Buffet has never had failing trades, then you need to correct your knowledge. It is not the absence of failure but persistence, the habit of reinvesting, and the ability to never make the same mistake again that has been the key to his success and many others similar to him in the field.

As a general investor, the world of finance may not be your cup of tea. You may not have the time and luxury to spend hours after hours looking at market trends. You may also not be at the advantage of making the switches in your investments as and when bad news comes. That cannot keep you deprived of the spoils of the market. The easy way to offset these risks is to diversify your assets. Slowly and steadily widen your portfolio and include a wide variety of financial products that lower your risk and help you take advantage of the upswing.

Beware-Whatever You Do Stay Away From the 'Trash'

This is a word of caution that you must always keep with you. Many times, you'll come across products that promise to act opposite their character. For instance, bonds are supposed to be secure products. You invest in bonds because you want a part of your money to always remain safe from the market upheavals. What if you invest in bonds that promise returns equal to stocks. If you come across something like that, it should smell fishy.

Bonds are purchased not because there is a dearth of risky products in the market but to ensure that in all conditions, a part of your portfolio would remain secure. If even your bonds start carrying the same degree of risk, then there would be no security for you. This can easily happen if you invest in junk bonds. If you are ready to give up safety for returns, then you may get fully invested in stocks where the possibility of higher returns would be even greater.

This is a distinction that most people tend to forget or undermine but shouldn't.

When you are investing in your future, reliability is a very important factor. It must always come before returns. Definitely, the dent of a percent or two in returns is going to affect your prospects, but that wouldn't be as significant as the loss of the complete portfolio due to poor choice of investments.

Some Portfolio Suggestions

I'd again like to reiterate that your portfolio must be based on your requirements and must address the four essential questions raised at the beginning of the chapter.

Given below are some of the portfolio distribution suggestions that can help you set your priorities and meet your investment goals at various stages of life.

For a Young Investor
Domestic Large Cap Funds: 50% Coverage
As a young investor with little knowledge of the market, large-cap stocks can give you the standing ground you need as they are comparatively stable and secure. They have lower volatility, and you also tend to get regular dividends.

Domestic Mid-cap/ Small-cap Stocks: 30% Coverage
These stocks can help you with an aggressive market strategy as the small and mid-cap stocks have a greater potential to grow within the same time frame. Although they are riskier than large-cap stocks because you have a major stake in the large-cap and time by your side, you can afford to take the calculated risk here.

Intermediate Term Bonds 20%
Usually, these are the bonds that have a medium-term maturity. This means that intermediate-term bonds may mature anywhere between 15 years. By the time these bonds mature, you'll have a good portfolio and experience of the market, and hence reinvesting your money into better growth opportunities would give better results.

Middle-Aged Investor
Large-cap Domestic Stock Fund 25%
This is a segment that would provide stability to your stock portfolio but also keep the doors of growth open. However, because by this time your portfolio would have grown bigger and widened its scope, you must divest a little and increase your presence in other securities too.

Small-cap/ Mid-cap fund 15%
This is the growth segment but also has greater risk. Getting too easy with this segment can be very risky, especially when you have time ticking fast. By the time you reach middle ages, even with the same percentage share of investment, the actual amount would have gone up, and hence even a 15% investment into this segment will keep the doors of rapid growth opportunities open. However, you must not raise your stake too high in this segment due to high uncertainties.

International Funds 10%
International funds provide you a buffer of growth. It has been noted that when the domestic markets perform well, the international markets are a bit slow, and when the domestic markets are slump, the international markets show rapid growth. Therefore, investing a little even in the international stock funds would give you the best of both the worlds.

REITs 10%
Real Investment Investment Trusts (REITs) are a different type of stocks that don't behave as usual stocks. They offer more dividend payments, transparency, competitive returns, inflation protection, and liquidity. However, the investments in REITs should always be conservative.

Intermediate-Term Bonds 20%
As usual, you can take intermediate-term bonds and keep your portfolio secured. Investing in intermediate-term bonds at this stage will give you the advantage of having a chance to make another change in your early retirement.

Inflation-Protected Securities 20%
Inflation-protected securities are good for investment in several respects. They ensure that your principal doesn't remain stagnant or get sacrificed by inflation. These are diversified funds actively managed by professionals. It is easier to get Inflation–protected securities than acquiring inflation-protected bonds, and you don't need to do anything to reinvest your returns as they can get reinvested automatically without any sales charge, and hence that also lowers the expense.

Chapter 17: Diversification

I'm sure most of you would have heard this term and would have an understanding of its meaning. It is only the importance of the term that gets overlooked.

Diversification is the simple principle of keeping your investment in various accounts so that they remain protected from any setback suffered by any specific asset.

This is an idea that might look counterintuitive to many investors who have just seen growth in any specific asset or who are highly optimistic about any such product.

They are not wrong to think that if they keep their money in that product, they might see better results within the same period.

They aren't wrong. However, a simple fact that they overlook is the outcome they might have to face in case the asset doesn't perform as per their expectations.

An ideal portfolio selection involves picking assets that have the potential to show rapid growth as well as those that are expected to move up at a steady pace. Diversification is one of the most important principles of investing.

You must remember that the most important reason for investing is not to earn more money but to preserve wealth for the future. You can't attain the objective of preserving wealth without investing it in a manner that everything doesn't come in danger at once.

If you look a few years back, you'll find that there was the time of the dot com boom. Even the technology companies that had nothing with them were performing well. People were buying in a frenzy as there was a fear of missing out (FOMO) in the investors. The dot.com companies looked like a cake, and every investor wanted to have a piece of it. However, we all know how that ended for the investors.

As an example, Xerox is a company that once knew no bounds. The stock price of Xerox kept rising and rising year after year. Within the ten years of the 90s, the price of Xerox stock went up from $25 to $159. Most people who hadn't invested in the company wanted to have a piece of this price.

Now, suppose you felt that the company was lucrative that the company already looked and invested all you had in stock. The price remained steady or fluctuated a little for some time. However, by the end of the year, you witness that the stock has started tumbling. It'd be prudent to take an exit, but you have all your money, or a major part of it invested in that stock.

Getting out of that stock at that stage would have cost you a lot. You decide to stick to that stock and wait patiently. You wait for a few months that turn into years, and after waiting for ten years, your total investment in that stock is worthless.

Now, some people may comment that getting out of that stock early on would have been prudent.

Others may opine that staying in that stock was a wiser step in general as any spring back in the stock would have helped.

As an investor, both the options had their use, but both were equally worthless for you in your current position. You had all your money invested in a single asset, and that was the cause of all the problems. If you had a small portion of your asset, the loss wouldn't have looked substantial, and you could have got out of it easily or allowed to deplete that account without sweating much.

The root cause of the problem lied in your heavy reliability in that particular stock.

It doesn't matter whether you are placing your money in a particular stock or a bond; if you have invested heavily only on one thing, your investment will always be at risk.

The trick lies in investing your money in a diversified portfolio and keep modifying it as per your age and requirements. When you are young and have a lot of time on your hands, you can be a little more aggressive in terms of investments and focus on gathering more money for a strong portfolio. As you advance in age, your portfolio must become more diversified and have a focus on stability and growth.

Reliance on segments through ETFs and Index funds should be increased in comparison to individual stocks and bonds as the risk percentage in them is even lower.

Chapter 18: The Benchmarks for the Best Investment Opportunities

Now that you have an idea about various investment opportunities that you may have in the money market, you might feel pumped up to put your money to work. It is very natural for any person to feel persuaded to earn money from money. There can be nothing better if your money can earn more money.

When about to invest, most people begin thinking of themselves as visionaries and want to take the riskier road that is more lucrative. You'll have agents and brokers singing the praise of such opportunities and giving guarantees of assured returns in a very short period. They can even vouch that they've invested their own mother's money in those products. Such products look lucrative, but they do not come under the standard definition of investing. You might feel tempted to give it a try and take the risk as mentioned by the legendary poet Robert Frost in his poem 'The Road Not Taken.' But, this is a mistake you don't have to make. There is a big difference between investment and gamble, and the point must be thorough in your mind before you proceed to invest even a dime in the market.

Invest Keeping Your Goals in Mind

This is a very important thing most new investors overlook. Let us understand this with the help of a story.

Suppose you are walking on a desolate road. You are thinking of your future and the things you have planned for.

It has been almost 15 years since you have been working. You have a 5-year-old child who is very bright. Your wife has always loved to go on a world tour, but the plan has been getting postponed due to financial constraints and the bindings of work.

The thing that's on top of your head is money.

- You'll be retiring in a decade or so. You'll need money for your post-retirement period, but you don't have much.
- Your son would be of the college-going age by the time you retire, and you'd need a lot of money even for that.
- You want to take your wife on a world tour, and you also need a lot of money, even for that.
- Retirement also means that regular income stops pouring in, and hence you'd want some source to compensate for that.

While you are thinking of all this and walking on the road, you see a man beckoning you. He tells you that he has a magical tortoise. If you keep that tortoise for a fixed period of 60 years, you could get diamonds from its belly. However, there are certain conditions. You can't sell it to anyone. You can't try to cut it open before that period, or else it will die, and you'll get nothing. It needs to be vaccinated every month, and the vaccination is very costly.

Do You Think That It is a Value Proposition for You?
There is no doubt in the fact that if the tortoise gives you diamonds at the end of 60 years and they are big, they'll be worth a lot. But, you'll be in your 90s by then. What purpose would the diamonds serve for you?

You'd need to pay for the vaccination every month. This is a steady cost that you'd add to your expense without the hope of a realistic return within a valuable period.

Your expected expenses are about to come within 20 years. If you are going to get your returns, what good would they be for you?

This is the first most important thing that you must look for in every investment. If an investment is not in-line with your goals, it is not meant for you.

Don't fall for investments with fancy results in unrealistic timelines. You must visualize your financial goals and invest as per those goals.

Most investments are much like that tortoise. In a premature state, they are non-transferable. You can't get profit from them before it is due. The final return is always uncertain in most investments. There is always a certain degree of market risk involved. No matter how secure any investment is, but you must not forget that there is always a certain risk involved. Not only the value of stocks can go down, but even the bonds can become worthless.

When you invest, you are putting your money for the future, and the future always has some uncertainties. But that is something that doesn't happen very often and unavoidable. However, not considering the time your investments are going to mature is a risk that you must never take.

Moral of the story, always put your money, taking into consideration your needs and long-term goals. If an investment is not going to give you the returns at a time, you may need it, which may not be the best fit for you. Such investments can be good for creating legacies for future generations, but they wouldn't mean anything for you.

The Period of Investment

This is another very important thing to consider in an investment. As we had discussed earlier, a very big portion of your investment would grow when you are not actively contributing to it. This doesn't mean that it'd stop growing at that pace if you keep contributing. It simply means that it'd continue to grow at a steady pace, even if you are not actively contributing to it. However, all your investments may not be of that nature, especially the ones that you begin at a later stage as they won't have the advantage of time.

Also, if you'd need money soon, i.e., short-term, it wouldn't be a wise idea to invest as you'd need to pull out the money at a fixed time no matter the market condition. This can lead to a loss. Therefore, if your outlook is short-term, saving is always a better option than investing. Keep your money in cash saving accounts.

Thinking of investing in stocks, bonds, or mutual funds is not a good idea for the short-term as you may not get the returns you are expecting. On the contrary, the value of your investments may even be lower.

Make an Investment Plan

Planning is always better than impromptu investing. It may sound complicated, and some people like to play as it comes, but believe me, it can be one of the best and most sincere advice that you may ever get.

Always remember that all investments are not created equal. Some investments have a very high risk to reward ratio. It means that they can grow very fast even in a short duration. These investments can give a boost to your overall corpus. However, they always carry high risk. Your total investment can even get zero. These investments are only good for younger investors as they have a lot of time ahead of them, and their risk-taking ability is high.

Some investments have a low rate of return, but they are more secure. These are very good for people beginning to invest late in their life as they can't afford to lose their money.

However, keeping all the money in only one type of investment is never a prudent decision. Choosing the correct portfolio that's diversified as well as customized to your needs is very important.

You must jot down your short-term and long-term financial goals, current liabilities, ability to contribute toward savings and investments, and then figure out a portfolio that not only gives you long-term returns but also has scope for rapid growth.

Selecting most of the security instruments such as stocks, bonds, mutual funds, ETFs, pension funds, Roth IRAs, etc. is always a good idea.

If you think that investing in all these would require a lot of money and you may not be able to take that much out, there is no need to worry a lot. As you move ahead with the book, you'll understand that it is not that difficult because you won't have to take out a lot of money and certainly not all of it, at once.

Are You Up for Commitments?

This is a question most new investors may ask themselves when they are about to begin investing. In the beginning, money matters may look very attractive and intriguing. But, you must understand that investing is a long-term commitment. If you choose an investment strategy in which you need to monitor your investments carefully, then you will have to devote some time to your investments regularly. This can start looking very demanding and tedious.

You can also choose to invest in mediums that do not require your active involvement, and you can simply keep investing and look for fixed returns at the end of the tenure.

Both kinds of investments have their advantages. The investments that require your active involvement can give you opportunities for rapid growth. Investment in equities falls under this category. But, even with equities, if you have a long-term view and you have done your research of the company well, you can invest for long-term and not bother about the fluctuations happening here and there.

Bonds, mutual funds, and pension funds are some of the investment types that do not require your active watch. First, most of these are managed by fund managers who are well versed in the market, and they are making adjustments on your part. Second, they have very low risk, and hence they keep giving you steady returns at the promised rate.

Therefore, the choice will always be yours. It is always good to invest with a long-term view and not bother about short-term fluctuations. However, you shouldn't sit with your eyes completely shut as the 2008 market crash showed that nothing is immune to the market crash, and hence, being watchful always helps.

Differentiate Between Investing and Spending

As an outsider, we all like to think that all the money we are investing in is going towards the retirement fund we are planning or the cherished dream you have. However, that's far from being true. There are charges, fees, commissions, taxes, brokerages, etc. that remain hidden.

When you invest money in a mutual fund, a part of that money goes into the maintenance of that mutual fund. It means that the money would be the fees of the fund manager for managing all the securities in that fund. The brokerage firms charge commissions, and the government takes taxes. This is a piece of information that's cleverly kept concealed by most beneficiaries or presented in a way that it doesn't look like a big deal.

Here, you must understand that there is nothing wrong with charging fees for the services. The fund managers managing your fund are highly experienced people, and there would be a cost of their expertise. But, the important thing to watch is whether this fee is a bit too much.

When investing, it is always better to look deeper into such expenses as you can be getting the same product at a lower cost.

Going for the cheapest option is always not the best option in investments. But, it is also not prudent to splurge. Whenever you invest in any product, clearly ask for the expenses, charges, and commissions you'll need to pay. Always remember that there is every possibility that you might get a discount or a similar or better product at a better price somewhere else if you are looking keenly.

All That Glitters Is Not Gold

When you point your nose towards the cash market, you may see big earning opportunities. You'll be splattered with rags to riches stories where people made fortunes overnight. There will be brokers or agents telling you about the money you can make and the golden opportunities just at an arm's distance. **You must not pay any heed to them.**

This is not to say that they are lying or deliberately trying to push you towards a debacle. They are simply trying to sell high-risk products that may or may not work. However, in any case, the agents or the brokers will get their commission. But, you may be left with resentment and a financial setback.

There is a clear difference between investing and trading. Investing is done in products that are steadier by nature. They may not seem to fetch big returns in the short-term, but when left over a long period, you will get good results.

Trading is generally profitable in high-risk products that have great volatility, volume, and movement. The traders try to reap profit no matter which side the tide moves. This is riskier, time-consuming, and requires a lot of experience and knowledge.

Therefore, as an investor with a long-term perspective, you must stay from high-risk products that glitter like gold as even the sand in the desert gives the same impression.

Chapter 19: Weighing Risks and Returns

Of Course, There Is Risk in Investing

This is probably **The Most Important Chapter** in investing.

When we talk about investing, we talk about big numbers. It is always motivating to think that if you invest $1000 today, you could get several multiples of it when you retire. That's your money working for you.

We like to calculate compounding interests at a rate of 10% and above. However, We do know that the numbers are just projections, and they do have the potential to go up or down.

We like to believe that the market has been consistently rising after the market crash during the great depression. Therefore, it is safe to assume that it'll continue to do so. However, we fail to take into account the debacle of 2008. We just like to remember the way it sprung back after the crash and not the time it took to make the rebound or the number of people who lost all their savings and investment during that period.

Everything in this world has a risk, and the risk in the money market is higher than anywhere else.

Everything may be going fine. You might wake up on a sunny morning, sit for your breakfast, and hear the news that the market has begun to fall or has already crashed. This has happened in the past, and it can very well happen again.

But, the bigger question is, should you be concerned about it?

If you are an investor, you should be concerned about it.

Investing doesn't mean locking your money in a blind pit for years. Although you are expected to wait for longer and not fear minor fluctuations, you'd still need to be watchful of the market events so that nothing devastating happens.

You must understand that even the safest securities can become worthless, and that's a possibility with everything in this world. It is very important that you clearly understand the percentage of risk involved in any kind of security and invest accordingly. If anyone tells you that any security comes without any risk, then that person is lying or cheating you.

Before we discuss anything further, you must clearly understand the term 'Risk' with greater clarity.

Understanding Risk

We'll not get into the technical definitions as they tend to get boring and have very little appeal.

In layman's terms, the possibility of loss is called a risk. Now, as you know, there is a risk everywhere. Nothing comes without risk. Either it is the personal life, professional, or finances, the risk is always there.

In personal life, there is a risk of deception, adultery, lies, and deceit. People look for the best life partners they could think of, but still, marriages fail. In professional life, you could have a bad boss, unprofessional coworkers, and clingy clients that may not let you succeed. You could always change the job, but the risk of getting the same or worse in the next job is always there. In the same way, even your investments are not free from risks.

No matter how safe you've played, there is some degree of risk always involved with everything.

The most important trick is to understand:

- The Degree of Risk Involved
- The Factors Increasing the Risk
- The Reason Behind Taking the Risk

Let us understand this with a simple example.

We all need to go out for work. Now, we all know that there is a degree of risk involved in driving. There can be unforeseen circumstances and unfortunate events. However, that's a reasonable risk if you are driving properly, following all the traffic rules, and not driving rashly.

Investing is also similar to driving. If you invest safely in good securities, don't take unnecessary risks, and don't feel tempted by flashy opportunities, there is a very low risk for you.

Investing with clear objectives and keeping the risks in mind is the most important decision you'll have to make every time you think of investing.

Choice of Securities: The kind of securities you choose would determine the type and extent of risk you face. Some types of securities offer faster gains with short turnaround time. Such securities naturally carry more risk than the ones with lower or steadier return securities.

Let us take the example of two main securities **Shares** and **Bond**

Now, there are two main ways you can earn money through investing; that is:

1. By owning an asset and selling it at a higher price later on. **Shares** are the medium to own a part of a company
2. Lending your money to a person or an entity and earning interest on your money. **Bonds** are the medium to lend money to a company

Shares: When you invest in shares or stocks of a company, you become a partner for the percentage of shares you hold. If the company makes a profit you gain, if the company goes in a loss, you lose. Some companies also give timely dividends, and you earn extra money from that. If the company whose stocks you own is performing well, has made some breakthrough, invented something that is very useful, or has started outperforming its competitors, the value of the stock can begin to rise very quickly, and you can make a lot of money in a very short span.

Monster Beverage Corp is a good example. It was a beverage selling company that was doing steady business since the 1930s. However, in 2002 it introduced its flagship drink 'Monster,' and the sales of the company rose from $92 million in 2002 to $2 billion in 2012.

If you had bought 1000 shares of Monster Beverages sometime in 2005, it would have cost you around $600. If you had allowed it to stay there, in January 2020, the value of those stocks would be around $65,000.

However, this is the best-case scenario. Owning shares of a company also means owning a share of the loss.

For instance, if you had invested in 1000 shares of TechnipFMC, you'd have paid anywhere between $44,000-$45,000. Although the stock continued to rise decently for a couple of years, it began to witness a decline in late 2014. After ten years of keeping your money in the stock, the value would be around $8,000. This is a loss of around $36,000. This might look scary, but it is also a possibility.

Let us look at a bigger name. Xerox is a big enough name if you are a 90's kid. There would be very few who wouldn't have heard this name. There was a time when xerox became synonymous with photocopying. This was a brand that was growing like anything in the '90s, and if you had invested money in it in the early 90's you would have made a fortune by the end of the decade. But, if you invested in the late '90s and kept invested, you'd be very sad.

Xerox Stock:

Jan 1990: $23 and kept rising steadily and

July 1999: $156 from here the downfall begins

For a decade, the Xerox shares rose and then began to fall hopelessly. By the end of the year 2000, the price of Xerox stock was $12.

However, if you thought that investing in such a stock that had fallen, so much was going to do any good. If you had invested in 1000 shares of Xerox in 2001, you'd have paid $18,000. However, in June 2020, the stock was trading at $15, and that puts the value of your stock at $15,000.

We have looked at three scenarios.

Best Case Scenario: The stock price increased in value from $600 to $65,000 in 15 years.

Worst Case Scenario: The value of stock plummeted from $44,000 to $8,000 in 10 years in the case of TechnipFMC.

Stagnant Case Scenario: The value of Xerox stock has remained in the same range in the past 20 years. It was priced around $15 in 2001, and the current price of the stock is also in the same range.

The risk to reward ratio in stocks is very high. There is a great chance that you could make a lot of money on your investment, but there is also a great risk that you may lose a big chunk of your investment.

Now let us look at bonds.

Bonds: When an entity issues bonds, it is just asking for loans. When you invest in bonds, you get an interest payment at a fixed price for a fixed tenure.

For instance:

Suppose Monster Beverages had issued bonds with an interest of 5% for 15 years. You'd get $50 every year for $1000 invested in it and your principle of $1000 after 15 years. This means your return on the investment after 15 years would be $750 in the best-case scenario.

However, even in the worst-case scenario, let us suppose that the company kept failing and didn't have a good product. But, it somehow kept itself afloat and made its interest payments for 12 years before filing for bankruptcy. Even in that case, it would have given you $600 in the form of interest payments, and a big part of your principal amount will be recovered after the assets of the company are liquidated as part of the process.

If the company keeps performing moderately, in that case too, the company is liable to make the interest payments on time and return your principal amount at the end. This means that even in the case of moderate success, your money is completely safe, and you are going to get the assured returns.

What this essentially means is that the bonds are comparatively safer, but the rate of return in the case of bonds is limited. No matter how wonderfully a company performs, the investor is going to get only the promised returns. Whereas, in the case of stocks, the investor can have a part of that success as the value of the stocks will increase.

However, this is also true in the case of an unfortunate turn of events. If the company fails to perform, the stocks can become worthless. But, even in that case, the value of bonds may still be recoverable to a great extent.

Therefore, an investor has to make a crucial decision in what to invest and how much to invest. If you keep all your money invested in bonds, you'll have very limited returns at the end of the tenure. That might be a very secure option, but it isn't the best option. Investing in stocks is risky, but if you invest everything in stocks, your investments may remain insecure all the time. You'll have countless sleepless nights over the uncertainty.

Minimizing the Risk Through Diversification and Rebalancing

These are the two words that may act as 'Mantras' of success for any investor.

Diversification: When you follow diversification, meaning you invest in a variety of securities like bonds, stocks, mutual funds, ETFs, you get the cushion that everything wouldn't fall at the same time. This means that even if one or two securities perform poorly, there would be securities that remain unaffected. Hence, your overall returns would remain secure.

Rebalancing: This is the act of periodically monitoring the volatile securities you have and adjusting your investments. Investing is done with a long-term perspective, and small price changes are not taken into account. But, if there is some major news about any stock or if you see that the particular stock has been consistently performing poorly, then getting out of it is prudent and important. As an investor, you can't sit with your eyes completely shut about such investments. Remaining aware of such events and making appropriate adjustments is called the act of rebalancing.

Investing will always have that inherent risk, but it can be brought down significantly by keeping these two mantras in mind. You must have a very diversified portfolio as per your financial goals and risk appetite. If you are young, you will have the liberty to take more risk, and hence you can devote a big part of your portfolio to stocks that have the potential to outperform the market and a smaller part to slow-growing but safer securities like bonds. However, if you are in the middle-ages, your investment portfolio must be more conservative as you don't have the advantage of the time by your side, and hence taking bigger risks can be devastating.

Not understanding the factor of risk in investing is a sin.

Never Underestimate the Power of 'Fear and Greed'

In the world of finance, fear and greed are two of the most powerful emotions. These are the emotions that drive the markets. Stigmatizing these emotions is not a good thing as without them, there would be no profit and no loss. However, both these emotions can be deadly for an investor.

As an investor, your outlook should be longish, and hence you have no reason to believe that something is going to outperform the market or sink without reason. This is the reason investing is done with a neutral outlook and average expectation.

When you are about to invest, you must have a return expectation and go for the securities that promise that kind of return. There is no reason for you not to invest in things that promise an extraordinary result, but such investments should be moderate. As an investor, your focus must be securities that are growing at a steady rate.

Individual stocks have the potential to grow extraordinarily; however, they are also more likely to take a nosedive and render your investments worthless.

You must understand that fear and greed are the emotions good for traders. These emotions keep the market ticking, and you see the constant rise and fall in the prices of stocks. However, this is not what brings profit to an investor. An investor gains money when a company performs well on a steady basis. Big traders and market manipulators can even bring a spike in the prices of worthless penny stocks, but they can't keep them there, and hence an investor must not become influenced by such rises and falls.

When you invest, you must look at the fundamentals of the company and not its technical charts. Going for mutual funds is even safer as the portfolios are selected by fund managers having years of experience in the field, and they understand risk better. Not only this, they only invest in stocks that have a good reputation, and hence the risk in the investments goes down even further.

If you are keen on investing in the stocks of any specific industry, going for ETFs in place of an individual stock is even better as an industry, on the whole, is less likely to collapse than an individual company.

Fear and greed are powerful emotions that drive the market and the traders, but they aren't good for investors. As an investor, you must focus on reinvesting your returns and compounding interest, and you'll have a peaceful time.

This is probably **The Most Important Chapter** in investing.

When we talk about investing, we talk about big numbers. It is always motivating to think that if you invest $1000 today, you could get several multiples of it when you retire. That's your money working for you.

We like to calculate compounding interests at a rate of 10% and above. However, We do know that the numbers are just projections, and they do have the potential to go up or down.

We like to believe that the market has been consistently rising after the market crash during the great depression. Therefore, it is safe to assume that it'll continue to do so. However, we fail to take into account the debacle of 2008. We just like to remember the way it sprung back after the crash and not the time it took to make the rebound or the number of people who lost all their savings and investment during that period.

Everything in this world has a risk, and the risk in the money market is higher than anywhere else.

Everything may be going fine. You might wake up on a sunny morning, sit for your breakfast, and hear the news that the market has begun to fall or has already crashed. This has happened in the past, and it can very well happen again.

But, the bigger question is, should you be concerned about it?

If you are an investor, you should be concerned about it.

Investing doesn't mean locking your money in a blind pit for years. Although you are expected to wait for longer and not fear minor fluctuations, you'd still need to be watchful of the market events so that nothing devastating happens.

You must understand that even the safest securities can become worthless, and that's a possibility with everything in this world. It is very important that you clearly understand the percentage of risk involved in any kind of security and invest accordingly. If anyone tells you that any security comes without any risk, then that person is lying or cheating you.

Before we discuss anything further, you must clearly understand the term 'Risk' with greater clarity.

Chapter 20: Tracking Progress and Rebalancing Positions

Tracking and Rebalancing are two important, very important terms that must be clearly understood by every investor. There will be several places where you might feel that the instructions are contradictory.

For example:

It is advised that an investor must not get affected by day-to-day fluctuation in prices. By tracking the progress of your funds, you'll be doing the same.

It is also advised that an investor must allow the securities to grow at a steady pace and must not change the overall portfolio allocation. However, by rebalancing, you are being asked to do that only again.

A simple answer to this lies in the fact that the real fun lies in the fine print.

The two principles mentioned above are very important, and the process of tracking and rebalancing do not come in the way.

Let us understand the terms with some clarity:

Tracking

By tracking the progress of the assets in your portfolio, you are not required to keep a strict vigil of every movement of your funds. Tracking your progress in investing means monitoring the performance of various assets periodically or when any asset class crosses any benchmark set by you.

You must understand that your assets are not static. Leaving them unattended for a decade or so can even be devastating. Let us again come back to the example of Xerox stock. It was an asset that was outperforming everything around it.

It was a big company, and no one expected that the same stock could reach a stage in a decade from where reviving it would become impossible, and the company may begin thinking of liquidation of assets. However, that happened.

In the early 90s, the Xerox stock started gaining and kept rising unchecked for a whole decade. If you had bought the Xerox stock and forgot all about it until your retirement in 2020, you'll be staring at an account in ruins.

Whereas, if you had been periodically supervising your account, you would have noticed the steady fall of the Xerox stock. It was an unmistakable phenomenon.

Would you have been able to get out of the stock in time?

This is a question that can't have a straight answer because the possibilities are many, and that would have depended on your rebalancing theory. But, one this is sure that Xerox stock wouldn't have stayed in your account for that long.

We'll come to this point once again when we are done explaining rebalancing.

Tracking the progress is the act of periodically monitoring the progress of various asset classes you have in your portfolio.

Through tracking, you get a clear idea about the assets that are outperforming in their asset class and the underperforming ones.

The best rule in finance is to buy when low and sell when high.

Most traders try to do this, but no one has the vision to know what can be termed as the highest point, and in the same way, no one can tell whether the asset has touched bottom. Therefore, the best way to determine is by studying the current trends and understanding the support and resistance levels of that asset.

There is no way you can catch the peaks and valleys, but you don't even need to. You simply need to find if any of your assets is nearing its resistance or support levels in its class, or is it outperforming or underperforming.

Rebalancing

Rebalancing is the crucial act of keeping your portfolio distribution in the same ballpark range. What this means is that the portfolio you have chosen for yourself is as per your risk tolerance and financial objectives, and it is in your interest to keep it that way. But, you can't expect your assets to keep behaving in a certain way all the time.

There may be some slow performing assets that begin performing superbly. Although this is a good thing, it will create an imbalance in your portfolio balance.

You must maintain the right balance of fast-performing and secure assets. If your stocks have outperformed the market for some time, it will increase the value of assets in that class, and your portfolio would begin leaning on the wrong side.

You might think that an over performing asset is good news, and there is no reason for you to get rid of an outperforming asset. This is where you are wrong. The asset which is going up can't keep going up indefinitely. There is gravity. It will return to mean. When that happens, you will have lost the advantage, and then there is no confirmation that the asset may stop at its original levels. There can be a further correction in pricing.

This is the reason whenever there is an asset that has outperformed and has risen well above its range, and you must rebalance your portfolio by selling that asset and reinvest in an underperforming asset.

Rebalancing gives you the advantage of selling high and buying low.

Need for Tracking and Rebalancing Assets

Tracking and rebalancing assets help in keeping the portfolio balance healthy. Every portfolio has a financial objective. Apart from providing you financial gains in the long-term, the use of a portfolio is to provide you peace of mind.

If you have selected a portfolio that's leaning more on the safer side, the value of stocks increasing above the ballpark range can begin giving you sleepless nights.

If you want your portfolio to grow faster, you'd want to keep more aggressive assets in your portfolio. If the secure assets have outperformed somehow, shifting the profit to buy aggressive assets will be a good long-term plan.

This is a big reason why tracking your progress and rebalancing is always a good strategy in healthy asset management.

Now, let us get back to the Xerox stock and whether you would have sold it if it had been in your portfolio.

A golden rule for portfolio management is to monitor your assets periodically and set a maximum growth perspective. If an asset has outgrown that limit, it is always better to sell that asset and reinvest in assets that may have underperformed in the same period

It may look like a losing proposition, but you must not forget that no asset will keep overperforming forever, and neither would keep lying dormant. Making these adjustments periodically would give you a chance to reap the surges and a chance to strengthen your portfolio balance.

As an investor, you must keep in mind that your portfolio has a steady target, and even if an asset is giving more than that, you can't be sitting over it forever. Such assets may turn out to be nuisances that may just cause distraction.

Section - V
The Right Amount to Save?

Chapter 21: It All Depends on Where You Stand At the Moment

The answer to 'how much to save' would be different for every individual. If you have just begun your job and you are in your early 20s, you have a long career ahead of you, and hence even if you begin saving a little, you'd be able to save a lot, and we have discussed that already in Chapter 4. If you are in your mid-30s, you might have to save considerably more because you won't have that advantage of time and early beginners have. You will also have better risk-taking opportunities as you still have time left on your hand. However, a person thinking of investing a decade later would have very little time left on his hands. There will be no scope for risky ventures as you have your retirement very close. The amount for investment would be considerably higher, and yet the expected returns can't be expected to be very high.

Therefore, the answer to 'How Much to Save' is case-specific. Several factors would determine the amount you must begin investing at that age. In general, the more you invest, the higher would be the result. However, this is not the answer you might be expecting here.

Your Age

As you can understand, this is probably the most important factor in investing. The sooner you begin investing, the easier it would be for you. You can begin investing even a little part of your income, and the total, in the end, would be big. But, age is not only important for the amount of investment you'd need to make but also for the type of investment you can make.

It is common for young investors to invest more aggressively because they have time by their side, and hence they can make risky investment decisions. This not only means they have a chance of getting higher returns, but their overall investment ability would also increase if they choose to reinvest the earned capital from their investments.

A person with advancing age would have a lower chance of taking a risk and hence would need to invest more to get the same kinds of returns.

Years in Retirement

Sixty-five years has been getting used as the standard age of retirement. However, it is not prudent to be fixated on the idea of 65 being the ideal retirement age. People can now easily work past that age or at least remain capable of earning in some way or the other.

If you can simply extend the age of retirement when you begin using your retirement fund, you can help in increasing the amount you can have to spend. The more time you give your fund to earn interest, the heftier it would get. Therefore, even when you are unable to contribute to your retirement fund, you must allow it to grow for a little longer. The more time you give it, the higher returns you can invest.

Estimated Rate of Return

This is another important factor that you must keep in mind. All securities don't give the same rate of return. While bonds may fetch the lowest returns, investment in stocks, ETFs, and mutual funds generally grow much faster. It is very important to keep these factors in mind.

Keeping your investments in a diversified portfolio helps you in getting a better rate of return on an average. For instance, if you have 10% of your money in high-risk securities and some of them give you a greater return, 30% in medium-risk and they give moderate returns and 60% in bonds that grow at a steady pace, you will have a secured portfolio that will have the potential to grow at a good rate without much risk.

You will always have the choice to increase your investments in the type of securities you like as per your risk-taking abilities, and this would help you achieve your expected rate of return.

The simple rule is never to invest fully in only one type of security, as that can be risky. In your early 20s, you can invest more in stocks, mutual funds, ETFs, and IPOs and expect faster returns. However, as you grow, you can begin investing in more stable securities and begin reinvesting the earned capital regularly.

What Do You Plan to Save for

This is another important factor that would determine the amount you'd like to save. Earlier, life expectancy used to be lower, and hence people needed less to save. But, thankfully, that has changed with the help of modern medical science, and you can easily expect to live until your late 90s. Therefore, you must keep in mind the money needed to sustain it for that long. If you want to leave something for your future generations or would like to support others, your investments would need to be higher.

On the internet, there are several calculators available that can help you in calculating the average contribution for getting the expected return at any specific age. You will simply need to fill in the expected rate of return, the years you have before retirement, and the inflation rate, and you'll get the amount you'd need to save every month.

These numbers are always changing, but they help give you a general outlook. Hence, you'd find yourself in a better position to make the correct decision.

The various asset class that you may choose don't come with static returns. Most have some volatility, and hence your returns can always go a little up or down. Still, you will get the idea that can help you in becoming more confident about your decision.

Section - VI
Efficiency Is the Key

Chapter 22: The Investment Decision Needs to Be Safe, Profitable, and Convenient

It is human nature to strive for the best. We don't even want to settle for the second-best. Do you remember any time when you purchased something, went a few steps ahead and saw that the same thing was available for a better price? This happens all the time, and we all feel cheated.

Now imagine you had gone to a thrift shop to buy a painting to hang on your wall. The shop owner had two pictures. One looked old and battered while the other looked much better. However, you wanted to pick the old and battered painting as it had a more antique look. But, you went against your better judgment and bought the painting that looked comparatively new. To your dismay, you found in the news that the painting you left was an old masterpiece of some great painter, and the new owner was getting value in millions for that painting. Wouldn't that feel defeating?

We all want to go by our gut feeling. We have been told to trust our instincts. We all always want to have the best. These may be true for life in general but not in the world of investing.

We all want to strike gold every time we invest even a single dollar, but we all know that it isn't possible. You may feel pumped up listening to the examples Warren Buffest and Goerge Soros, but what you fail to listen to is the knowledge they had and the patience they have shown. If you feel that whatever they picked turned out to be gold, you are wrong. They picked up things and then turned them into gold, and when it was accepted as gold, they sold it.

As an investor, you will never have the time, patience, and experience to find gold in the dust of the financial world. What an investor can do the best is to find the securities that have been performing steadily on average and include them in the portfolio.

Listening to your gut can be devastating in the stock market, and hundreds of thousands of people that have lost their money in the stock market will vouch for that. The money market is not the place to go by the hunch you have. It has its mood, and even the wizards of the market sometimes fail to predict that mood. Therefore, you must not try to attempt that.

Most people believe that they can ask the advice of the experts as they know more about the market and then invest. It is another misconception that you must get rid of. Either they are your friends or some agencies that boast of providing tips about the best-performing stocks and multi-bagger stocks, you must stay away from them as they won't do any good for you.

Investing is a long-term decision. It is a decision you will be making for your future. It does require some of your time in the present. Going for the lot as a whole in the form of ETFs or mutual funds is the best as it saves the time and effort that goes into selecting a stock. However, if you are keen on investing in any specific stock, you must devote time to study its historical performance, the dividends it gives, and major news events about the stock and their performance on the stock. These are the things that can help you in determining whether that stock is good for taking a long-term position. Do not get swayed by the recent uphill movement of the stock as they are temporary, and a stock that has rapidly begun moving upwards would witness a correction very soon, and as an investor, you wouldn't have the time or knowledge to get out of it then.

Finding all that with some accuracy is a task that's not possible even for the most experienced. However, you can't take a risk with the hard-earned money you are investing for your future.

The best way out is to focus on three main areas:

Safety: You might have your heart on a specific stock, and there might be a hundred good reasons for that stock to perform, however, is there a way for you to be sure about its performance? You might say that we can't be so sure about the performance of any asset. However, that's not completely true. You can never be too sure about the performance of any specific company, but you can always be sure about the future and performance of any specific industry or the index in general. ETFs (Exchange Traded Funds) and Index funds are the two asset classes that can help you in investing without having to bother about the performance of any stock in particular. There is no chance for an index or a complete segment to fail overnight, and besides minor ups and downs in the prices, it has been observed that the overall performance of index funds and ETFs is generally even better than actively managed funds. Therefore, you can safely invest a portion of your money in them and take a sigh of relief.

Profitability: The main objective of investing money is to earn a profit. However, that can become very difficult when you have to pay a lot to manage those investments. A major issue with most actively managed funds is the maintenance costs and service charges. When you invest your hard-earned money into something, you'd want all of that to go towards your future. But, that's not how it works with actively managed funds. Safer investment options like index funds and ETFs are better even in this area. You can invest in them at no brokerage cost or commission, and the maintenance charges are also negligible as compared to the mutual funds, and hence you can be sure that your money is going in the right account. More money invested for the future also means more returns in the end. You already know even smaller amounts added from an early age can make a difference in the end. The same would also happen with the money you saved from brokerages, commissions, and fees.

Convenience: As we had even discussed in the past, the idea of tracking the assets, going deep into the money matters, and chasing the stocks looks better in the beginning. However, soon you'll realize that although it is intriguing, it is time and resource-consuming that could be utilized better in other areas. Investing is done so that your money can earn money for you. If even you have to work with that, then the real use and advantage would look compromised. All investments must have your initial involvement when you are selecting them, and you must also keep a watch over your investments, but daily trading is not something that would suit you as an investor, and hence it must be avoided. A big advantage of the index funds, ETFs, and mutual funds is that they offer greater convenience. You can invest in them and just relax. Even if you keep a watch over your investments periodically, that will work in your interest perfectly.

Chapter 23: Do Not Fall for the 'Financial Wizard' Misbelief

As an investor, the temptation to actively get involved in the trading process or actively buy and sell assets would catch up sometimes. There is nothing unnatural or abnormal in this. Money is one of the most lucrative things in this world, and when you get an opportunity to make money fast, it gets irresistible.

However, this is the stage you need to get alert and refrain from trying to manage your investments by watching over the trades actively. There is no doubt that you might do good in some trades. Quickly getting in and out of shares may even help you make some quick bucks. However, you'll need to keep in mind the crucial fact that correctly timing the market every time is an impossible task.

Do Not Try to Time the Market

There is no way you can find the peaks and valleys every time. It doesn't take too many mistakes to turn your complete portfolio worthless.

Trading and investing are two very different things. As a trader, you are trying to find smaller margins and a high number of trades. As an investor, you are trying to stay invested in a stock and earn from the dividends and returns. By trying to time the market, you'll be defeating the whole purpose.

Investing is done with a long-term perspective. If the stock or asset in which you are thinking of investing is in the average price range, then there is no use trying to find the lowest price within that range. The longer you wait, the more difficult it will get for you to enter the market.

Don't Try Beginner's Luck Too Hard

You may strike gold in the early trade and start considering yourself as a financial wizard. There is no problem in having an air about yourself, but problems may arise when you try to push your luck too hard. Even if some of your trades do good, you must not get into active management of your assets. Frequent buying and selling of assets not only involves costs, but it also means greater risk as you may get panicked by a sudden movement of any asset in an undesirable direction.

You must understand that investments are made with a long-term perspective, and until and unless there is a significant and steady decline in the price as well as any specific news, you need to stay invested in that asset. Frequently trying to shift your assets can also mean loss.

Learn to Swim with the Tide

It is very adventurous to take the road less traveled by. However, in the financial world, it can be very tricky. If the whole world is optimistic about the future of a stock and even the reports of that company are also saying the same, your gut feeling that something is wrong with the company wouldn't change anything. The market likes to move where the volume is.

Most people like to quote Warren Buffet, advising the investors to be fearful when others are greedy and greedy when others are fearful. Although that sounds great as investment advice for active traders and experienced investors, it'd be very difficult to follow for a general investor. Fear and greed are powerful emotions, and they do dictate the day to day trading, but an investor must stay unaffected from them as that would make the investor switch investments very too often, taking away the advantage of time.

As a general investor, a large chunk of your money should be invested in safe assets and the remaining significant other in asset classes like index funds, ETFs, and mutual funds where the onus of selecting the specific stocks is not on you.

Section - VII
Managing the Costs

Chapter 24: Understanding the Expenses

Spending and investing are two very different things; however, they'd be presented in the same tone many times. As a bright investor, it'd be a task for you to find out the amount of your money that would be invested for your future and the amount of money that you'd need to spend just to invest that money.

Expenses in investing are hidden in plain sight. It is a deception that works most of the time.

However, most investors simply agree to pay the high expenses because they don't realize the enormity of these charges.

Every year, the investors in the US alone pay more than $300 billion in brokerages, advisory fees, legal fees, customer fees, sales loads, marketing expenditure fees, processing expenses for the securities, commissions, and transaction costs.

Try to imagine the money that goes towards fees and expenses. You must keep in mind that the aforementioned $300 billion is just the expense towards fees and brokerages, and it doesn't include taxes. You'd be paying taxes over and above this price, and we'd be covering that in a separate section.

The people in the financial world also need to survive, and hence charging a fee for their services is nothing wrong. However, there should be a limit on the fee that's reasonable, and most of the time, that limit is crossed without giving a consideration.

Charges, commissions, and fees are the precious part of your fund that would go directly into the pocket of the fund manager or broker. Most of these charges are recurring, and hence it is very important that you clearly understand these charges and try to avoid them wherever possible.

Such expenses don't come along just with mutual funds, but they are also present with equities, index funds, and ETFs. But, the charges levied on each kind of product are different, and the costs would also vary from your broker to broker.

Therefore, an investor needs to know about the real cost and the cost being asked. If possible, you must try to get the cheaper option. Most people believe that higher costs bring you quality products; however, in the world of investing, that may not be true because the product is always the same, and the seller or the broker may differ. Therefore, if you are a bit selective about the broker, you can save a lot on the costs.

When investing, it is very important to understand all the costs associated with the product. Most of the time, only the visible costs are explained, whereas many hidden costs are never explained to the investor. This would also have an impact on your overall return because, as an investor, you are always calculating your returns on the amount you have paid from your pocket. Awareness about expenses is also important for dealing with such costs.

Most investors trust their brokers on their word and do not pay attention to the prospectus. This is a fatal mistake, and you must read the prospectus carefully.

Although some fees are given with greater clarity in the prospectus, some charges are not very clear even in the prospectus.

The following chapters would help you understand all such charges in detail.

Chapter 25: Understanding Various Fees Covered in the Prospectus

Front-end Sales Commission or Sales Charge

When you invest in any mutual fund, you need to pay a front-end sales commission or the sales charge. This is not a uniform fee. The broker may charge a different fee from every customer. Generally, the fee is higher for smaller investors and reduced for people investing larger amounts.

It could be around 5% of the total amount you invest. A 5% cut may not look a lot, but you must remember that it is just one of the costs of the many that may come, and it is going to come from the total amount you are going to invest.

If you invest a total of $100,000, then $5,000 would simply go towards the sales charge. Dreams shatter when you begin calculating profit on the total amount. For instance, let us imagine that the annual rate of return on your investment is 10%. Most people would imagine that their total corpus would become $110,000. However, they are wrong. Their total investment was just $95,000, and their return would be 9500, bringing their total to $104,500. As you can see, that's $6,500 less than the expectation while the cost was always in front of your eyes.

The broker would easily justify the cost as the charges for facilitating entry into the portfolio, but you'll be left with a substantial cut in your invested amount.

However, important this is the fact that these costs are not fixed, and you can very well bargain about this cost.

It is also important that next time when the broker explains the expected returns on your investment, you look at that after deducting the cost that would go towards the front-end sales commission, also known as 'Load.'

Back-end Loads or Deferred Sales Charge

This is the charge you pay when you are getting out of a mutual fund without holding it for long enough. The period would vary from product to product, and so would the back-end loads.

The back-end load is also around 5% for the first year. It keeps coming down by one percent every year. So, if you stay in that mutual fund for more than 5 hours, you won't have to pay the back-end load, also known as the deferred sales charge.

Here, it is also important to know that although longer stays in mutual funds can save you from the back-end loads, you may still have to pay the 12b-1 fee every year, and hence there will be a cost.

Another issue that would need attention in the prospectus would be the amount on which the back-end loads would be levied. This means that while some mutual funds charge the back-end load on the initial invested amount, others charge it on the total at the time of withdrawal.

Therefore, staying informed of the conditions in the prospectus is always helpful.

No-load Mutual Funds

This is the age of no-load or brokerage-free transactions. However, there is no free lunch in this world. Anything that comes with a free-tag always has something in the underwriting. You must understand that maintaining mutual funds needs active management by fund managers, and hence it can't be free. When a mutual fund comes with the free tag, it usually means that you'll need to pay several fees to meet the expenses, and some of them would be visible while others may be hidden.

Fees Charged are:

Purchase Fee
This is the fee usually charged from new shareholders when they enter into a fund. This fee is around 1% of the purchasing cost. The rationale behind this fee is to cover the cost of the purchase of assets of the share of the new investor.

Redemption Fee
Like you pay a fee to get into an asset, you will also need to pay to get out of it. This is the sales fee with a different name. You will have to pay the redemption fee when you get out of a fund; however, this fee doesn't go to the brokers but the long-term buy-and-hold investors. The purpose is to penalize short-term investors and

Account Fee
If at a time your account balance falls below the minimum required balance, you may also be charged a maintenance fee. This is charged as the cost of maintaining the account for you.

Exchange Fee
Many a time, you'd want to switch funds even within the same group of funds. This is a common practice undertaken to increase earnings. However, it won't happen for free. Mutual funds charge a fee for exchanging funds. The objective of the fees is to discourage the practice of market timing, expensive fund transaction, and lower fund expense of long-term investors, but the impact is reflected directly on the balance of the investor making the switch.

Management Fee
This is a fee over and above the charges mentioned above, and it is charged for the active management of the fund. It goes to the fund's investment advisors and portfolio managers.

12b-1 Fees
Do you know that the food packages that say no trans-fat in the US are not free of trans-fat? The regulations state that if any food item contains less than 0.5 grams of trans-fat per serving, it can be written as trans-fat free. Most food items with trans-fats are tempting and don't fill you up. You can keep munching them forever. This means that even in a single sitting, you may eat several servings consuming several

grams of trans-fats that are very unhealthy for the heart. However, the food product manufacturers can still go unscathed by selling their products as trans-free because they haven't violated a law.

The same is the problem with No-load fund expenses. Even they charge fees to cover distribution expenses and various services provided to the shareholders. However, the SEC regulations state that any fund that charges fees less than 0.25% of the allocated fund can be termed as No-load funds.

Many times you may ask yourself whether something free is truly free. However, this is a fee that would be charged from you, and there is no way to escape from it.

Others
If you thought that charges have come to an end, this is a wake-up call. There would be several fees that may seem insignificant, but they would be present in the prospectus. They may not look much individually, but when you club them all together, you'll get to know the overall load you're asked to pay. The charges may come in the form of legal expenses, custodial expenses, transfer agent expenses, administrative expenses.

Although these are a part of the 'total annual fund's operating expense' and are needed, the problem begins when you are not aware of them fully, and you begin calculating your returns based on the money invested.

You can choose to go with a mutual fund that is explicitly asking for the expenses or with a no-load fund, but there is little possibility that you'll be able to avoid these charges.

The best way is to remain informed and read the prospectus fully so that you clearly understand the charges you'll have to pay and the kind of returns you can expect.

We are discussing the expenses in the mutual funds in such detail because they look highly attractive to the investors. They come with the assurance that they are getting managed by the fund managers with good financial expertise. However, understanding the cost of having them is also equally important because, in the end, it all boils down to the amount of money invested and the kind of returns received.

Chapter 26: Understanding the Fees Not Covered in the Prospectus

Several fees are never mentioned in the prospectus. However, an investor has to pay those fees anyway. Every service has a cost, and there is nothing wrong with that. However, keeping the payee in the dark about that cost or taking them without giving a full disclosure is something that seems to be a more problematic thing.

Some of the hidden fees are:

Brokerage Commissions

Some brokers may charge a hefty fee while others may boast of working for you for free. However, on average mutual fund managers charge 0.38% on fund assets.

Spread Costs

This is another expense that remains hidden but gets charged on a mandatory basis. Although this cost doesn't go into the pocket of the broker or the fund manager, it surely goes out of the pocket of the investor, and hence it is a cost. The spread is the difference between the ask and the bid price of any security. This is charged by the market makers, and it may look insignificant, but the average spread cost is around 0.34%.

Market Impact Costs

This is another cost the investments in a mutual fund face. The mutual funds deal in securities on a very large scale. They are not trading nominally, and hence every buy of sell made by mutual funds needs to be large. This means while you can sell your assets at the prevailing market price, the same might not be possible for the fund managers due to the large size of the portfolio. Therefore, when buying, the fund managers need to offer a higher price than the current market value to acquire all the stocks at a specific price from large sellers. The same is also a problem when the fund managers need to sell any specific asset. They need to sell it to specific buyers in large lots and hence need to offer a better price than available in the market.

Both scenarios mean that the assets are bought higher and sold lower. It is the exact opposite of what you'd like to do in the market. But due to the big size of the asset, it becomes a compulsion for the fund managers, and this can lead to losses anywhere between 0.5% to 20% of the value of the security traded.

If you think that any fund manager can avoid this, you are wrong as the market is anyway going to respond to heavy buying and selling, adjusting the costs. The fund managers can do that more proportionately. But, that is a hidden cost anyway that the customer doesn't get to know.

Wrap Fees

It has become quite fashionable to have personal attention. We are ready to pay a premium for that, and the same is charged by the mutual fund firms. If you want a fund manager to supervise your funds personally, you'll be required to pay a wrap fee of 2% or more on the total invested amount. This is the cost of having a personal money manager. No matter how lucrative and tempting that may sound, it is always a wasteful expense to pay twice for a money manager. When you invest in a mutual fund, your money is going to get managed by a professional, and seeking personal attention to your money is not going to do any good.

However, that's a bone most firms would throw, and people are ready to jump on it.

Turnover Cost

This is again a latent cost that goes out of the pocket of the investor, and there is nothing an investor can do or gets to know about. Turnover cost is the overall expense that takes place in switching securities within a year. It is a continuous process. As the prices fluctuate or the fund managers see a better opportunity in other securities, they make a switch. It is done for your best. However, this best doesn't come without costs. The spread costs for buying or selling the assets, brokerage commissions, market impact costs, and management costs are some of the expenses that might get added to the list.

On average, a fund will see a 100% turnover within a year. This means that in a financial year, at least assets worth the total value of the fund are switched. This cost comes heavily on the overall profit ration.

Funds with lower turnover are more profitable as their overall cost is low. The turnover cost can be asked from the brokers or seen on various websites. However, investigating it further would also help you understand the average turnover rate in a fund, and you'll be able to assess a mutual fund better.

Chapter 27: Spending Lavishly Matters- Finding Low-Cost Options

Why Do Expenses Matter So Much?

We have discussed the expenses in mutual funds in such great detail that you might have started wondering why do these expenses matter so much. The easy answer is that these expenses matter because they are going to affect your overall retirement.

Let us suppose the overall return on your mutual fund is 10%. This is a more optimistic projection, but let us work with this for now.

You begin investing at the age of 25. You invest for the next 40 years.

If your monthly investment amount is $300.

The final amount would be $1,665,104.44

Out of this, $144,000 would be the principal amount

The interest would be $1,521,104.44

You could make more than ten times the invested amount.

The expense cost in mutual funds is around 3.3% annually.

Now, let us suppose that you earned returns with the same rate, but 3.3% got deducted in expenses.

Now, the figure would stand out to be:

The total contribution would still be the same: $144,000

The total interest earned: $541,587.70

Your final amount would be $685,587.

As you can see, just a decline of 3.3% in total earnings can bring down your overall retirement fund by 60%.

As an investor, you need to understand that every penny matters. The more lavishly you spend on things that are not bringing any results of assets that have wasteful expenses, the more you'll stand to lose.

For a long-term retirement fund, the more money you can stash, the bigger would be your return due to the compounding interest.

Why Low-Cost Options Are the Better

Several low-cost investing options have a similar or even better rate of return.

When it comes to the rate of return, most people believe that trading equities can get you the best returns. However, that may not be entirely true. If you look at the facts, you'll find that even the most consistent traders don't have an average return higher than 6%. At the same time, the average equity investor is only estimated to gain by 4.25%.

This rate of return is higher in mutual funds due to the management by experienced fund managers. Yet, good stock mutual funds remain in the 10% ballpark range, and bond mutual funds linger in the 5% range. However, you must not forget the cost that this is the overall return, and the expenses will have to be deducted from these returns, and that wouldn't leave the figures looking so good.

You have low-cost investing options like the ETFs and index funds that have a high rate of return and comparatively lower risk. They also don't involve a lot of speculation and decision making on your part because you won't be selecting any company in specific but a whole segment.

Historically, 80% of the time, index funds have performed better than mutual funds in terms of returns. They have almost one-fifth of the expenses of the mutual funds and much better results. Even the ETFs have low-expense, and they can also be traded like shocks. If you don't have a lot to buy index funds, you can even invest smaller amounts in the ETFs.

Investing in stocks for the long-term is also an option, and that also doesn't involve a lot of costs, but that would always remain very risky if you do not know a lot about the company and keep a watch over the stock.

No matter what you choose as the investment vehicle, the asset must give a reasonable return and have lower costs so that your gains can increase.

Section - VIII
Escaping the Trap of Phony Opportunities

Chapter 28: Best Way to Stay Steady in Investing- Noise Cancellation

Someone Is Getting Paid to Show You Dreams of Financial Success

This is a catchy heading, but just don't go on the catchy phrase but look deep into the meaning. The world of finance is noisy. There is a lot of noise and commotion. Every agent selling a financial product would try to sell his/her merchandise as pathbreaking. Every time you have a chat with a financial planning agent, numbers would get thrown at you with lightning speed. No stone would be left unturned to prove that the financial product being advised is the best in class that has been designed till now and is tailor made as per your needs.

Show some courtesy, say some pleasant world, and excuse yourself.

Every day a new financial product comes that promises to overperform against index firms, and after a while, the buzz dies down, and the indices keep ticking.

The fatal mistake you can make is to get swayed by such products and act against your planned portfolio. You must keep in mind that until your financial objectives change in the long-term, there is no need to act against your portfolio structure.

The moment you create an imbalance in your portfolio by investing in such products, you will begin losing your sleep, peace of mind, and growth.

Even the greatest financial products that have had great hype and showed remarkable progress in the beginning ultimately got beaten by the long-term performance of the index funds and stable securities.

The basis behind such products is the active management of the fund, and that would lead to a high turnover rate. This means the overall cost, as well as the taxation load of the product, would also go up. Such products usually have high maintenance charges, and that also gets added to the cost. In the end, they are not immune to market forces, and therefore, one mistake in predicting the direction of the wind can lead to catastrophic results.

Your allocated portfolio is usually free of such disturbances. This is a reason it has better chances of long-term growth and stability at the same time.

The world of finance is highly competitive, and the people are there to earn big bucks at your expense. An agent that has sold you a product is immune to your loss or profit. If you make a loss, the agent would again get an opportunity to pay you a sympathy visit and sell you another star product holding the cruel market forces responsible for the debacle in the past. If the product last sold to you were a success, then the agent would pay a visit gloating in the successful selling you another product with better results. No matter which way the wind blows, the agent and the world of finance always win at your expense.

You must understand the motive behind selling such stellar products. They were never designed to benefit the end-user but to benefit the seller.

A financial product with low cost and steady returns is the best an investor can ask for. These two things together can help you in building your retirement fund without much hassle.

If you want to taste success in the long-term without having to spend sleepless nights worrying about them, you need to follow three simple things:

1. Design a simple but diversified portfolio with assets as per your need balanced in each segment
2. Learn the art of reinvesting. It is the magic behind a big fortune and not the numbers that rapidly tick on the ticker boards of the stock exchanges.
3. Tracking and rebalancing your portfolio is very important for the health of your retirement fund

You must understand that simplicity is the key to better investing. There are innumerable financial instruments out there, and some of them even work, but as a general investor, you will neither have the time and patience, nor the risk-taking ability and expertise to monitor them. What's even more interesting is the fact that in the long-run most such products are unable to outperform the index funds, ETFs, and other such simpler assets.

The mystical world of finance is not prospering by selling you lucrative products but by throwing mesmerizing pitches and luring the customers. If the financial planning agents had any magic trick to time or predict the market, they'd invest everything they could beg, borrow, or steal to make a fortune whose dream they are selling you.

The truth is, they are just selling you their forecast and expectation of the product working in the future.

The Bare Truth is:

It Is Impossible to Predict the Market With Consistency

This is a fact that no financial agent is ready to accept that no one in the market can predict the market with some consistency. There have been some examples where the market Moghuls have stricken gold every time they have invested in something. However, this is just half-truth. They started as simple investors and kept investing and increasing their portfolio. Slowly they increased their investing power to such an extent that any investment made by them brought a significant movement in the market beginning a trend. They are always the first to begin the trend and hence get the most of it at the lowest price. However, when they see that the trend is about to peak or near saturation, they exit. Even here, they are the first to make a move and hence get the best exit price. Their exit creates panic, and soon only ruins are left. They are not predicting the market trend but creating it. This takes power, consistency, and reputation. No financial product sold in the retail market for a commission can have all these three and yet be looking for customers. Also, such people never tell their plans to others. Therefore, if someone is trying to sell a product telling you that the product is going to bring path breaking changes, the changes are going to come just for the seller and not for you. For you, it would be another product with a high cost and similar returns that you could have received anyway without losing your sleep or money.

It Is Impossible to Time the Market

One of the biggest fancies humankind ever had was to look into the future. We all want to have the ability to see just a few minutes ahead into the future. That could change the whole world for us. We'd be able to bring remarkable changes and save numerous lives.

If you could predict the future just a few minutes ahead, you could be the one who would single handedly prevent most of the deaths caused by natural disasters like earthquakes, tsunamis, and fires. But, we all know that it isn't a possible dream. Only the people on the wall-street fail to understand that.

They feed their agents with the notion that they somehow have the magic, the power or the vision to time the market and hence they can help you in getting into a product when it is at its lowest and get out of it when it has reached its peak and is about to make a reverse.

It is practically impossible to time the market. Most people are doing guesswork or predicting trends based on technical analysis. However, this is a fact that the possibility of them going wrong is as good as you making a mistake.

Making a change in your investment decisions or portfolio allocation would be a very unwise choice.

But, it is also a truth that you can't escape them. They make use of aggressive marketing strategies, high agent incentives, and assurances of high returns to lure unsuspecting investors.

The agents are trained in the technique of convincing the customers, and the brokers keep them motivated by paying high commissions. Neither the brokerages nor the agents have anything to lose in this. The only person at the risk of losing hard-earned money is the customer.

Therefore, you must develop a thick skin against such agents and stop paying attention to them.

Chapter 29: 3 Golden Rules to Stick Closer to Reality

Finance is a highly motivated segment. One of the biggest motivations behind all kinds of work is money, and it runs as the blood in the veins in the finance segment. Hence, finding people who are just thinking of money and talking about money is not very strange.

However, you need to understand that personal finance and investing are not matters of enthusiasm but strategic planning. You can be and should be enthusiastic about trading as it is all about catching the peaks and valleys in the market movements. Trading is heavy when the markets are high and slow when the markets are low. Investing is a very steady function that keeps going on irrespective of the market trends.

You can consider trading and the market makers as the rabbit and the investor as the tortoise. The first leg of the race was won by the rabbit. But, you must remember that in the end, the tortoise wins the race, and it has been happening over and over again.

People trading in the market or involved in active management of their funds may have a lucky streak once in a while and get a return of 20 to 30 percent, but they will also get trapped in moments when they'll be losing much more. The average of such funds in the long-term is never more than 6 to 7 percent. Whereas, the average rate of return in long-term investing turns out to be 9 to 10 percent.

But, this is a world of aggressive marketing, and most of the time, it would affect you. It is hard to resist the temptations created by the market makers. Their bread and butter and the whole world of finance depend on such temptations. Many a time, they will succeed in influencing your mind and convincing you that they have better control over the numbers.

In such circumstances, you must remember these three golden rules:

1. You Need to Stay Away from the Marketing Bubble
2. You Need to Stick to the Basics
3. Knowledge is the Antidote to Silence Ignorant Noises

You Need to Stay Away From the Marketing Bubble

As a retail investor, you must always remember that you are a soft target for agents and brokers. This is the world where dreams sell. Let us get away from the world of finance for a moment and talk about health.

We all know obesity is a health nuisance. More than 70% of the adult American population is either obese or overweight. It is one of the five top reasons for more than 900,000 preventable deaths every year in the US.

Every sane American wants to get rid of the excess weight or prevent getting it in the first place. The answer to obesity is simple, and you need to watch what you eat, maintain healthy physical activity, and stay positive. Stress, inactivity, and disorderly eating are the three biggest reasons for obesity in the first place.

This is basic knowledge, and we all know it, yet the rate of obesity is increasing every year. The rate of obesity has tripled in the past 40 years, and a whole weight-loss industry has emerged that's busy convincing you that you can eat whatever you want and lead a life you like, only if, you eat their products, drink their magical potions, and do entertaining workouts on their machines.

This may sound illogical, but it is a fact that this sector has been successfully able to sell its pitch, and although it began just a few decades back, the annual turnover of this weight-loss industry is around $78 billion.

People know the cause of the problem, the reliable and cost-effective solution of the problem, yet they are ready to try such gimmicks just because they want quick results without much effort.

The marketing industry knows that consumers are gullible, and this is the weakness they try to exploit. They are always looking for soft targets who have the money to invest and the desire to earn quick returns without much effort.

If you think you have a thick skin, you are wrong. The more you entertain such thoughts, the more influence they'll have on your mind. The marketing is done on multiple levels with several pretexts. Somewhere it is about tax saving, whereas you'll find it more about rapid wealth building, so or and so forth.

The best way to escape such traps is not to entertain them as try to stay as far as possible from such thoughts. Rapid wealth creation is a mirage and a deception. It always works for trapping the unsuspecting victims, and it doesn't pan out well for them in the end.

You Need to Stick to the Basics

Keeping your basics correct is the best way to avoid the alluring trap of such risky investments. As an investor, the faster you understand and begin following the magic of compounding, the easier it would become for you to avoid such traps.

You need to understand the basics that wealth creation isn't an overnight job. It takes years of patience and perseverance to create wealth. If someone is showing you the dream of creating wealth overnight, there is no reason to believe such ideas.

The audio-visual aid has proven to be a highly effective tool to reinforce an idea into the mind of users. This is a reason financial products are launched with a big bang, and you'll see and listen to their advertisements very often when you get onto your TV, radio, or the internet.

The marketers are smart people, and hence they'll not only throw their products through sponsored programs and commercials. But, you'll also come across articles, educational programs, and books trying to upsell those products in organic ways.

It is a very effective marketing strategy because most of the retail investors fall for them, considering them as genuine advice.

In this age of the internet, it is very hard to differentiate between a piece of genuine advice or a planted one. The best way to prevent falling into such traps is to keep your basics clear.

You must understand the way the money market works and how it is going to affect you. As an investor, you have limitations of taking a risk and investing aggressively. You neither have the time nor the expertise to maintain a hawk-eye on the market and take advantage of the opportune time, and no one on your behalf can do it either. Hence, as an investor, it is in your best interest to keep things simple for yourself.

First, only invest in products you have complete knowledge about. Stocks, bonds, mutual funds, ETFs, and Index funds are easy to understand tools, and they have little complexities. Even if something isn't doing well, it'd be easier for you to track and correct it.

Second, you must also always maintain a balanced portfolio. Do not feel tempted by any overperforming product because that's not your goal, and hence you must always keep tracking and rebalancing your assets.

Third, your most sincere efforts should be directed towards keeping the costs low and taxes at their minimum. It isn't the bigger earnings but lower costs in the end that help you create wealth that can be of any use. Aggressively marketed financial products may have a higher return ratio, but they have even higher costs and taxes that can offset your gains easily.

The closer you are to the basics, the easier it'd be for you to avoid falling into the trap of dubious financial products.

Knowledge Is the Antidote to Silence Ignorant Noises

In the end, you must never forget that knowledge is the antidote to silence ignorant noises, and hence you will have to become a skeptic when it comes to big claims. If you have knowledge about the basics and you have done your homework, it wouldn't be difficult for you to reason well.

Most of the time, we don't get swayed by tall claims because their pitch is great, but because we want those claims to become true. This is just day-dreaming about a scenario over which you have no control.

Knowledge of the basics and deeper understanding of the investments is something that can help you in discerning facts from fiction.

If you feel that some claims are sounding too good to be true, in place of calling the agent to verify, sit down, and try to understand the basics about that product and try to find if it works on your parameters. If you think that the agent will be able to show you the dark sides or cons of that product, then you need to wake up fast.

There is nothing wrong with trying to sell one's product, and hence there is no force that can stop brokerage firms and banks from selling their financial product christened as the best financial product in the world. However, if you are equipped with the power of knowledge and reason, you'll be easily able to dodge such products and maintain the true course of wealth creation.

Section - IX
Surviving Taxes

Chapter 30: Impact of Taxes on Your Investments

Tax is a cost most people don't take into account as they feel they can't do much about it. This is a misconception that needs to get cleared.

There have been several long-term studies on the impact of taxes on the retirement funds, and it has been observed that the funds that have been kept in tax-deferred accounts have been able to gain at least twice more than funds that have in taxable accounts.

What this means is, if you kept funds worth $100 in a tax-deferred account for a period and gained $2100. The same amount kept in a taxable account for the same period would only fetch you $987. This clearly states the impact taxes can have on your retirement fund.

The after-tax returns would look bleak. For instance, the mutual fund returns for 15 years stood out to be an average of 5.4%. This is not very high but still looks decent. However, if you minus the 1.7% from this, leaving an after-tax profit to be 3.7%, the figure would start looking bad. But, this is a reality you'd need to come to terms with.

But, this wouldn't be the fate of every investment you make. If you invest in tax-efficient index funds and gain a return of 6.7%, the profit left with you would be 6.1% even after the deduction of tax.

The impact of the tax would also depend on the way the funds are managed. A study has revealed that actively managed funds tend to attract higher taxes in comparison to passive funds. On actively managed funds, the impact of tax can be 0.7 to 1.20% of the total funds. Whereas on passive funds, this impact is just 0.51 percent.

You must understand the specific parts of the funds that are taxed so that you develop a clear understanding of the ways to save taxes.

Capital Gains
The difference between your purchase price and the sale price is the capital gain or loss. If you sell something above the purchase cost, you have a capital gain. If you sell an asset below the purchase cost, you'll have a capital loss.

Realized Capital Gain or Loss
A realized capital gain or loss is the actual profit or loss that you might have realized by the sale or purchase of the asset. In mutual funds, the capital gain is passed on to the shareholders, and the information is forwarded to the IRS. If there is a capital loss, the same can be carried forward to offset future gains.

Short-term and Long-term Capital Gains
A short-term capital gain is a profit earned by selling an asset within 12 months of purchase. Short-term gains are taxed as ordinary income, and hence they get taxed at the highest marginal income tax rate.

Long term capital gain is a profit earned by selling an asset after 12 months from the date of purchase. Long-term capital gains enjoy tax relief. The maximum tax rate applicable to long-term capital gains is just 15%, whereas short-term capital gains can be taxed at a rate of 39%.

Therefore, simply holding on to your assets for longer than a year can also help you in dealing with a high tax rate.

Besides selling an asset, you also gain returns by means of earning dividends. You get dividends on shares, and that also gets included in your earnings.

Turnover is also an important factor in taxation. The higher the number of transactions, the greater would be the tax paid. This is especially true in the case of mutual funds that can have an overall turnover rate of 200%.

If you want to earn more from the money you have, your focus must be on saving the commissions and expenses, and that also includes taxes.

As an investor, your focus should be to look for gold. If you allow your assets to remain steady in their growth opportunities, you'll strike gold in the end anyway.

Chapter 31: Steps to Prevent Tripping Into the Rigorous Taxation Pit

Taxation is a complex subject with its arms sprawling in all directions. This is also a reason most people easily give up on taxes and become a victim of poor tax planning. However, even with the same set of assets, your tax liabilities can be completely different if you plan properly.

It is always prudent to go for the tax-efficient products; however, that may also not be possible all the time.

You can save a lot of taxes by taking the following steps:

Stay Away from Exotic Assets

When you begin considering investing, you might be approached by several advisors with exotic assets that offer things like an annuity, insurance wrapper, shelter, etc. As a golden rule of thumb in finance, if you don't understand the term with greater clarity, you must not pay heed to it. Such complex products may work well for the people well-versed in the world of finance and taxes, and they'll not bring anything other than trouble for a common investor due to their complexity and lack of understanding.

As an investor, your focus must be on looking for a simple product that you understand well, as it will help you in planning for the taxes.

Your objective should be to buy assets that have lower costs and fewer expenses.

High Turnover and Short-term Capital Gains Can Be Bad News for Tax Management

Most investors don't realize it in the beginning, but assets that are giving profit in the short-term may not bring as much profit as you may think. As explained, a high turnover of assets has its expenses. But, those expenses may not look much in the light of profit you are gaining. However, at the end of the year, when those profits get taxed at the maximum tax rate, the fun flies out of the window. You must also keep in mind that not only you'd be required to pay the maximum federal tax rate, but you'd also be liable to pay the state as well as municipal taxes.

Playing your investment as short-term trades will not only have a bad impact on your portfolio, it'd also have an impact on your tax statement.

Carefully Plan for Taxable Accounts

Taxable accounts can be a big headache for most investors. Taxable securities get taxed at maximum applicable tax slabs, and your profit diminishes. Avoiding tax may not be possible, but it is possible to buy certain investments that are practically free of federal taxes. Individual municipal bonds are such assets that can help you not only avoid federal taxes but even the state taxes. The rate of return on these bonds may be slow, but if you carefully compare the after-tax yield of certain taxable securities and the municipal bonds, you'll find that the latter has a better yield in the end.

Tax-loss Harvesting

Profit and loss are part of the financial world. However, tax-loss harvesting can give you a chance to compensate for your loss in the market. It is an opportunity to save taxes of the same amount.

For instance, imagine you have suffered a total loss of $5000 in any asset by December. There is nothing much to do here as you are already under loss. Now, you can choose to keep the asset and wait for the prices to recover, or you can simply choose to get rid of the asset and recover whatever is left. This may look like a complete loss of $5000, but it isn't.

If this was a loss-making asset, you might also have some profitable assets. If there are assets with you which have gained $1000 in profit, you can use the tax-loss for offsetting the gain. This would leave your remaining loss to be $3000.

There is a provision to use a maximum of $3000 to reduce the reported income on the first page of the current income tax return. In this way, you can offset a large amount of loss by tax-harvesting.

In the unfortunate event that you suffered even more loss, you can also use that as the 'capital loss carryover' to be adjusted in the next year's return.

Be Selective About the Placement of Your Assets

Proper placement of assets in the required accounts as per their taxing frequency is important. You should maintain one taxable account and a retirement account. Both accounts will have different taxation slabs.

You can place your aggressive investments in the taxable accounts as the chances of facing losses would be higher in such an account. Any loss incurred on the assets can be used for getting tax compensation through tax-loss harvesting.

You can place your long-term investments that are going to give high capital gains on maturity in the retirement fund so that you can get the tax relaxations.

Go for Low Tax Investments Like ETFs and Index Funds

Mutual funds are a popular investment option, and a large number of people trust them. However, there are some issues with mutual funds that can make them a big taxation headache.

First, many mutual funds are traded actively, leading to a turnover percentage much over 100%. This would increase the tax load on you.

Second, mutual funds can have unrealized capital gains that can put you in a taxation spot without having any profit at all. Their overall profit margin in comparison to the expense is also on the higher side.

ETFs and index funds, on the other hand, provide you a better investment opportunity. They are cost-effective, tax-efficient, require very little active management, and their overall return percentage is also high.

Section - X
Investing Psychology

Chapter 32: Persistence and Perseverance Win the Game of Investing and Not Precision

Most people believe that because the world of finance is so complex, it would be ruled by geniuses. Therefore, banks and brokerages are easily able to lure investors into believing that they'd be easily able to fetch them great results.

Although one shouldn't hold anything against intelligence, there is enough data to demonstrate that it is not the brain but persistence that helps you make wealth.

An interesting example of this is the performance of the Mensa Investment Club for over 15 years. As you may know, Mensa is an exclusive society that comprises of individuals with the highest IQs in the world. Logically, the members of this group would be able to map the market better and would have a deeper understanding. However, it was observed that while the S&P Index gave an average return of 14.9% within the same period, the average rate of return on the investments of this club was 2.5%.

You may think that there is no cause for intelligent people to fail in investing. As there are numbers and numbers all around and intelligent people are good at them. Fortunately or unfortunately, whichever way you perceive it, investing is not a complex game. It is fairly simple in its functioning and behavior. The real problem begins when intelligent people try to mess with the pace and principles of investing.

Intelligence and IQ are good only for trading where you need a lot of analysis and tracking. Trading is a game of predicting the direction of the wind within split seconds.

One of the biggest problems with intelligent people in investing is that they keep challenging their thoughts and forming biases.

Intellectual bias is a good thing for predicting immediate risk, but investing is mostly done in safer instruments, and when you begin analyzing them with biases, you are bound to feel compelled to make frequent changes in your investments, increasing the expenses and affecting your returns.

Some Common Intellectual Biases

Base Rate Neglect: Every intelligent person thinks that he/she has the supreme ability to spot an opportunity. When an asset begins to make a move, the first instinct of such people is to pounce on such opportunities. However, the market has shown us umpteen number of times that all crucial information is always included in the base rate, and there is nothing extraordinary being spotted by you.

Making sudden moves inspired by sensationalism is the base rate of neglect. Affected by this, you only try to look for the information already being fed to you and fail to see other factors like the fundamentals of the company or the asset, which will have a deep impact on the long-term behavior of any asset. That is the only thing that must concern you.

Recency Effect: This is another fallacy people develop. We quickly begin forming biases around recent events. If a segment has shown improvement in returns recently, we begin looking at the whole segment as promising. This was the reason people even invested in dot.com companies that didn't even have a real product. However, it didn't affect people as they just wanted to believe that if they have invested money in the segment, they will make money from it.

We all know how that fared for the investors in the end when the dot.com bubble broke.

An incident doesn't signify a trend, and that must be clear to every investor. If something is earning money rapidly, it won't continue doing so. You won't have the knowledge when it begins to come down all of a sudden.

Endowment Effect: This is another problem that affects most people. When some things are performing, we tend to believe that they'll keep performing endlessly and increase our reliance on those things to dangerous levels. We forget the basic principles of diversification and put all our stakes on one thing. This never works out well.

Keeping your portfolio well balanced and diversified is a simple principle of intelligent investing. Still, bright people often overlook the influence of their newfound confidence in any specific product.

Fear of Loss

Fear and greed are big emotions that drive the market. As an investor, you can't have greed, or else, you won't remain an investor but become a trader or sorts. However, fear is an equally devastating emotion when it comes to investing.

While in the previous point, we talked about the problems caused by the confidence of the intelligent people, loss aversion is also an equally damaging emotion.

As an investor, you'll always have a fear of losing your hard-earned money. This is a reason, investment portfolios are always so balanced and leaning more on safety rather than growth. However, you must not forget that the market is a volatile place. Therefore, no security can keep moving unidirectionally. Therefore, ups and downs in the prices are common and should be expected.

However, people with extreme fear of loss begin making rapid changes in their portfolio as soon as they see any signs of loss or slowdown in progress.

This is a step you must not take as it can be very damaging in many respects.

You must keep in mind that investing is done with a long-term perspective, and ups and downs are already factored in the returns. You do not need to make changes in your portfolio that can be damaging impatiently.

A Tendency to Overanalyze Everything

This is another problem factor that can influence your investments. Some people get so deeply engaged that they begin overanalyzing their investments. You must understand that you do not have influence over the turn of events, and hence speculating too much about the future is not going to help.

You'd need to calm your horses and learn to let the investments be. Although tracking the progress of your investments is a part of your portfolio rebalancing activity, it must not become your idle time activity.

Fault finding in the portfolio can lead to unwanted panic, and you may begin overthinking, overstating, and over speculating the results.

Chapter 33: Achieve Peace of Mind by Preventive Action

Our subconscious mind is much more powerful and active than we'd like to believe. The strongest emotions we have aren't a result of the thinking of the conscious mind, but a product of the unconscious mind. Fear and greed are also such emotions.

Fear and greed can become dangerous emotions because they can elevate your threat perception or force you to lower your guard too much. Both of these situations can be fairly dangerous in terms of investing.

You can try to fight these emotions or struggle with suppressing them. Whatever you do, eliminating them is not possible because they are a part of our mental makeup.

Having these emotions all the time can be a harrowing experience as they never allow your mind to rest. Once an individual begins having these thoughts, the process of overthinking begins, and the thought process spirals out of control.

People begin feeling stressed and lose the calm they had. Some people also develop anxiety, and issues like poor sleep regulation and insomnia develop in some cases.

Once these things happen, desperate attempts begin to calm the mind, drive out the stress, and bring peace.

You must understand one thing; if you are trying to win over your emotions, you are fighting a losing battle. There is no way you can win over your mind. The struggle is futile if it is to be done in this way.

Money is an important asset, but it isn't everything. You'd need to learn to be calm. You'd need to cultivate positive emotions that can replace emotions like fear and greed. This is the only way you can have deep calm.

Attempts to Eliminate Emotions Is an Act in Futility

If you have your money invested in an asset, and its prices are going down, it is natural to feel anxious. It would make you fidgety, and you'd begin questioning the basis of the decision to invest there. All of these are natural reactions. If you think that there is a way to prevent such thoughts or eliminate such thoughts, you are looking for the wrong thing.

However, it is possible to not worry about the prices of an asset if it is only a small part of your whole portfolio. Loss of even a single penny is a loss anyway, but if that penny is lost in thousands, the pain would be smaller.

Diversification and balancing of the portfolio are simple solutions for the frequent anxiety attacks that you might be having due to sudden price movements.

You can't eliminate emotions, but there are easy ways to deal with the causes of those emotions and address them in effective ways.

Avoidance Doesn't Work

There are several ways to look at a problem or to overlook them. Some people like to stick their necks in the sand like ostriches and pretend they didn't see the problem. This doesn't solve anything. A basic difference between trading and investing is that the tensions in the former don't last very long, and the results are clear very soon. Whereas in the latter, the results come very late, and the fear keeps eating at you. This is a reason the assets in the investment portfolios need to be chosen very carefully.

A bulging and imbalanced portfolio is a serious risk, and while you may choose to unsee the risk, your mind knows it, and it won't let you be at peace. Not dealing with a problem doesn't lower the risk of that problem; on the contrary, it increases the risk several times over.

If you want to be at peace with your investments, you'd need to ensure that your portfolio is not causing the anxiety that you feel.

Section - XI
Tips and Tricks for Investing

Chapter 34: 7 Major Myths About Investing That Are So Wrong

Investing is a subject most people don't understand with clarity. Not because it is hard to invest but solely because it belongs to the finance segment, and people perceive it to be complicated. This makes it easy for others to create myths and misconceptions about the whole section.

Trading myths are easy to burst as traders need to be active and have to study the markets continuously. However, that's not the case with the investors. The investors may have very little engagement and interest in the market, which helps the misbeliefs get strengthened in mind.

This chapter would discuss the seven most common myths about Investing.

There Is a Secret Recipe for Success in Investing That Others Don't Know

No, there isn't. This can be the most common line in the sales pitch of the investment advisors, agents, or brokers that you might hear. Investing is simple, and there is no secret recipe in investing. It prospers by the magic of compounding interest, and those that are perseverant in investing can create wealth in the end.

If anyone is pitching you the secret recipe pitch, you are about to be sold an average product that'd come with an outstanding angle. There is a secret recipe for KFC's chicken, there is a secret recipe for the secret ingredient X in coke, but there is no secret recipe in investing.

The simple trick in investing is to begin early and remain committed with the habit of investing regularly.

There may be times when some assets in your portfolio would underperform, and the average returns would be comparatively low, but there would also be times when the average returns of your portfolio would be higher than most products. This is how the market works.

If you are tracking the progress and rebalancing the assets in your portfolio, you wouldn't have to worry about any secret recipe as you already have it.

Eagle-Eyed Wizards Win in Investing

This is another self-suiting myth created by banks, brokerage firms, and investment advisors. Most eagle-eyed wizards have better earnings only for themselves because they are earning from the commissions you pay. The returns in the market are always average, to say the best.

Investing is not about luck or precision but consistency. The more consistent you are about investing, the better returns you'll have in the end.

Investing is an art that very few people genuinely understand is just a catch-phrase of marketers, and it has no depth. You can easily spend your money on several products without much knowledge or experience and get good returns.

Therefore, if you are a regular retail investor who wants to earn steady returns, you simply need to stick to the basics. You'll have the kind of returns expected.

You'd Need a Lot of Money, to Begin With

We have dealt with this myth in detail at the beginning of the book. There can't be financial investing without money. However, you don't need to have a lot of it, to begin with. There are several ways in which you can start investing at the primary level. You can keep diversifying your portfolio as your investing capital grows, and you begin to get returns of earlier investments.

The worst you can do with investing is not to invest at all and keep waiting for a lot of money to get accumulated. While you do so, you'll be losing on the interest that the money could have earned for you.

If you want to begin investing, do it now. No matter how small the amount is. Take a small step forward so that you have an inspiration to take the next level.

Investing Is Cumbersome

Most people fear that they don't have an understanding of the way the market works, and they don't even want to invest their time and energy into it either. They feel that if they think of investing, they'll have to figure out a lot of things, and that would affect their regular course of time.

Investing can be as cumbersome or as relaxed you want it to become. It is a fact that if you want to ensure that your money is not going into a bottomless hole, you would have to look deeper. Therefore, some time is essential to know the products you are considering for investment. However, this engagement can be as limited as you wish to keep it.

This simply means, if you don't want to invest your time in investing, you can take financial products like mutual funds, index funds, and ETFs. With mutual funds, you already have a fund manager to manage the funds. Index funds mimic the whole index, and hence there is no need for active management of these funds. They even have low operating costs and tax benefits. ETFs can also be traded, and they are cumulative shares of the whole segment.

Therefore, if you go this route, there would be no need to invest time in managing your money. Your investments would work on their own, and if you look historically, all these products have given better returns on average than other financial products.

You Must Invest in Stocks to Get Bumper Returns

This is also a myth that needs to be broken. Although it is a fact that stocks have a better probability of giving better returns because the value gain in the stock gets transferred to the shareholders too, it is also a fact that the loss also gets transferred in the same manner.

If stocks can gain 20-50 % in a year, they can also lose even more than that. This means that a person investing in stocks also has an equal probability of losing money. Investing is not about quick-big gains but steadier gains over a long period, and for that, there are many options like bonds, index funds, and ETFs.

It Is a Game of Experts

Some agents like to boast about the brilliance of financial advisors on board and the way they can change the performance of the fund.
They'd go lengths to tell you that your money wouldn't look back once you invest it in their product.

You must ask them to take a chill-pill.

The brilliance of financial advisors is a gimmick. Your guess in the market is as good as mine, as far as market movement is concerned, when equipped with the same facts. However, the price of the stock already covers these factors, and no one has the power to predict the market.

Therefore, there is no reason to fret that you don't have a subscription to their advice.

All you need to do is to keep investing and reinvesting the profits steadily into the market. You'll have substantial gains in the end. God willing, you may even have a better rate of return than those advisors if you don't keep switching at every market move like them.

Investing is more a game of patience than skill. You'd need to remain watchful and observant to take necessary steps in unprecedented times, but an involvement more than that is not required.

The Higher the Risk, the Higher the Reward

Higher risk is not a guarantee of better returns.

This is a proverb that is true in some measure but presented most of the time incorrectly: higher the risk, higher the chances of loss. Risk is not always proportionate with the reward you might get, but the loss is always proportionate and severe.

This proverb is presented as if higher returns are a guarantee of higher returns.

When David went to fight Goliath, the risk was high, if he had lost, Goliath would have killed him, and that was certain. However, the reward wasn't certain. David was fortunate that he was able to target the vulnerable areas, but that wasn't a certainty. Several factors could have made him miss the mark or hit at a place where the damage wouldn't have been so severe.

When you think of investing in something risky, you must keep in mind that the risk to reward ratio may not be proportional, and the risk is not a guarantee of the reward. Investing in risky assets should always be limited as caution doesn't work that well when you are talking about the long term. There are too many eventualities that can offset your caution.

Therefore, investing in stable securities and keeping the risk proportionate to your risk tolerance and financial objectives is very important.

Chapter 35: Major Investment Obstacles You May Face

Undefined Financial Goals

Investing must always be done with a defined financial goal. If your objective is not clear, you may lose your commitment midway. This is just for your dreams in the future.

You must also have clearly defined goals about the kind of assets you want to have in your portfolio or the type of balance you want. Most investors who do not have clear financial goals about their portfolio balance get disoriented in the middle and start taking erratic decisions.

As I have mentioned in the book, it is very easy to come in the influence of the so-called financial advisors, and you may want to give their product a try. There is no problem in that as long as you keep the asset allocation in mind and do not create an imbalance in your portfolio. This is easily possible if you don't have a defined goal for your portfolio.

Your objectives from your portfolio must be clear, and you would have to follow it to the letter if you want your financial objectives to get accomplished.

Low Control Over Expenses

You can have a six-figure income, and you may still not be able to find a way to find money to invest a penny. This is not a hypothetical situation but a reality for many. When people hear about the kind of wealth they can create in the end, they feel highly motivated to begin investing, but when they look deep inside, they are unable to find the money to do so.

Your investments, as well as your returns, are dependent upon your investments, and they are directly linked to the type of expenses you have. You can save for investing even if you earn a few hundred dollars a month. This is a reality, and we have discussed it at length at the beginning of the book.

Management of expenses is the basic task if you want to have money to invest or a sizable retirement fund in the end.

Some people don't pay adequate attention to this aspect of investing and continue holding a portfolio that has assets with high maintenance costs or keep assets in accounts where high taxation reaps off most of the profits.

Keeping expenses of both kinds under control is very important for maintaining a healthy investment portfolio.

Getting Swooned By Exotic Opportunities

This is another fatal mistake that a very high number of investors made. If you had asked any regular investor in the '90s to invest in bonds or financial instruments with low returns, you would have simply got a scoff.

People were getting 15-20% returns from their certain stock investments as those stocks were the hot potatoes of that time. The more some investors earned on paper, the more other investors got inspired to invest their real money in those stocks.

The frenzy reached a point where even if you had stock but no office or product, even you could sell them in millions. People felt that missing out on such an opportunity was a mistake, and there could be nothing better than to invest in those stocks.

People had almost forgotten that a stock that's witnessing an upswing would also have a downturn.

This happened as soon as the new millennium arrived. Millions of people lost their money that was not even their savings or investment but realized after selling their assets simply to have a piece of the pie.

As an investor, make it a rule not to get swooned by such exotic opportunities. If you must have some of those, you must also ensure that this doesn't create an imbalance in your asset allocation.

One mistake in this regard, and you may have to regret your decision for very long or at least will lose your peace of mind until the balance is restored.

Trusting the Soothsayers

We have discussed this even earlier. In the finance world, you'll get countless people who'll claim to have predicted most booms and would ask you to invest in the product they believe is the best. You must find the earliest opportunity to run from that place as it is always a trap for an investor.

If I knew a product that could give me a 20-30% return for sure, I'd mortgage everything I possess to ensure I have the maximum funds in it.

This is just not possible. Even the best astrologers, psychics, mathematicians, and statisticians haven't been able to do that with any consistency.

Even I can read the books and analyze all the stats and tracks of the past and feel that I could have predicted them accurately and then miraculously fail when tested in real life and say it was by a chance of some force of the market.

Predicting the market isn't possible, and if it had been possible, the soothsayer would be sitting under seven locks predicting the market and making gains.

Never invest your hard-earned money into something just because they say that it is the best opportunity, or they have a gut feeling about it. When it comes to financial predictions, the gut-feeling is almost always wrong.

Overconfidence

One thing that you should never be in the market and that's overconfident about any specific asset. A fact that's a universally accepted truth is that the markets are volatile all over the globe. You are investing because you expect the prices to go down;

however, at the same time, there would be someone placing the bets on the markets going down. The market works both ways.

Hence, expecting the market would always behave in one way is childish or immature.

This is a reason to never become overconfident over any asset ever. Always diversify your assets no matter what. While it is true that an asset will never keep moving in the same direction always, it is also equally true that all the assets or products in the market will not sink at once. If a product fails, people withdraw their money and begin investing in another.

A time when stocks would perform poorly, other products would surely work because this is the nature of the market.

A person who isn't very confident with one product would keep the eggs scattered in various baskets and would have a better chance of surviving in place of the hustler who thinks that he is always in complete control.

Always remain suspicious of the ability of your assets to perform, and that's why you must have a diversified portfolio, so a large number of assets are always out of danger of market volatilities.

Don't Lose Your Sleep Checking and Rechecking the Performance of Assets

This is a problem many investors face very often. There are two categories of people who mainly face such issues.

1. New Investors: They are just checking out of curiosity. They want to know how the assets are performing, and they feel good to know that they are going to create wealth in the future. This is harmless fun, and there is no problem in indulging in it once in a while. What good is money if it can't even make you happy and confident.
2. The Anxious Lot: These are the people who begin checking their accounts even if there is slight movement in the market and begin losing their sleep if the markets are volatile or choppy. These people are at serious risk of losing all their capital due to incorrect decisions. The investment portfolio of such people must be shouting safety and balance, but they'd have the highest percentage of risky assets that are always volatile.

Every investor must understand that the main function of having an investment portfolio is to bring safety and security about the future so that you can sleep at night with peace. But, if even your portfolio itself is giving you sleepless nights, then you have certainly made a drastic judgment error in selecting your portfolio.

Periodic progress tracking of the portfolio is a good habit, but that shouldn't be too frequent because then you'll begin feeling anxious about every move the market makes.

You must understand that various assets in the portfolio are placed to absorb such shocks, and a balanced portfolio is capable of dealing with these issues.

If you check it very often, you may become anxious and have the urge to get rid of underperforming assets or buy the overperforming assets causing a serious imbalance in the portfolio.

You must maintain the sanity and sanctity of the portfolio.

Inability to Take a Beating

This can be a bit touchy subject, but it is equally important nonetheless. We all want to have the spoils of the war, but in our victory, forget that someone has lost a war at the same time, and once in a while, that can even be us.

Market comes with no guarantees, and hence even the most secure asset can fail. Who had ever thought that a giant like Enron would fail all at once? It was a company whose employees also preferred investing in its stocks. They lost their jobs as well as their capital, all at once.

The purpose of quoting this example was just to explain that any company, no matter how grand it is, can fail miserably. There are times when even the banks fail. There are countries where even government bonds fail at times.

However, that doesn't mean you can't have a comeback, or everything is lost. Even the most balanced portfolio can also see a loss, but that doesn't mean that it always happens that way.

If it ever happens, you must restrategize and reinvest.

Conclusion

Thank you for making it through to the end of this book, let's hope it was informative and able to provide you with all of the tools you need to achieve your goals whatever they may be.

Investing is a prudent decision that must be made as early into the career as possible. Most people believe that one needs to earn a lot of money to be able to invest. This is a misconception that I've tried to break with the help of this book.

At the beginning of your career, if you could just save as little as $10 a day by cutting down any expense, you'll be able to build a substantial portfolio for yourself a few years down the line. Taking out $300 is not a lot to ask. You can even take that out from your monthly payout because some people might think that moving a big chunk from the salary can put a lot of burden on them.

Investing is a habit that needs to be cultivated. It is something that'll not only help you keep your present organized, but it would also ensure that your future remains secure.

There are a lot of people who don't want to cut down on their expenses in the present for a future that's uncertain. This is a conclusion that has no basis. Based on this logic, working for the whole month to get the salary at the end is also asking for too much. There is too much uncertainty involved, as they may never reach there.

Investing is a habit that can help you have a safe and comfortable retirement where you'll not have a dependency either on the support from the institutions or someone else. Not only this, but you'll also have the power to live your life on your terms and fulfill all your financial objectives.

This book has not only discussed various tools you have to help you invest your money but also the way you need to formulate your investment strategies and the ways to prevent setbacks.

The book has explained the various hurdles you might face in the path of safe investments and steady growth and the ways to overcome them.

Selling investments to invest further is also a tricky subject that needs detailed understanding. The same has also been discussed at length.

Investing is a process that must go on. However, there may be times when the markets are choppy, and people are fearful. The book has covered the topic to help you understand the ways to deal with the situation.

This book has tried to present a solution to all your investment-related questions so that you can invest with greater confidence and success rate.

This book has solutions presented in a simple and easy to understand way. It has given you the key ideas that are needed to make them work for you effectively.

I hope that you will be able to gain full advantage of the information provided by this book.

Finally, if you enjoyed this book, please let me know your thoughts with a short review on Amazon. All that you need to do is to click the blue link next to the yellow stars that says "customer reviews." You'll then see a gray button that says "Write a customer review"—click that and you're good to go. It means a lot, thank you!

Bourke

www.ingramcontent.com/pod-product-compliance
Lightning Source LLC
Chambersburg PA
CBHW051757200326
41597CB00025B/4584